100 MUST-READ

PRIZE-WINNING NOVELS

Nick Rennison

B L

Bloomsbury Publishing Plc

3 5 7 9 10 8 6 4 2

First published in 2010

Bloomsbury Publishing Plc
36 Soho Square
London W1D 3QY
www.bloomsbury.com

A CIP catalogue record for this book is available from the British Library

ISBN: 978 1 408 12911 1

Available in the USA from Bloomsbury Academic & Professional,
175 Fifth Avenue/3rd Floor, New York, NY 10010.
www.BloomsburyAcademicUSA.com

Typeset by Margaret Brain, Wisbech, Cambs
Printed and bound in Great Britain by CPI Bookmarque, Croydon, CR0 4TD

CONTENTS

ABOUTTHISBOOK

This book is not intended to provide a list of the one hundred 'best' novels ever to have been awarded a literary prize. Given the sheer range of literary awards, the variety of works of fiction which have won one or more of them and the unpredictability of individual taste, any such list is an impossibility. Instead I have chosen one hundred prize-winning books to read which I think will provide a wide-ranging introduction to the pleasures of contemporary fiction

Some literary prizes date back many decades – the French Prix Goncourt, for instance, is more than a century old and the American Pulitzer Prize for Fiction has been around nearly as long – but the kind of media coverage they now attract is a more recent phenomenon. For this reason I have chosen to make my choice from books that have won prizes in the last thirty years. All one hundred main entries are books that have been published since 1980.

The individual entries in the guide are arranged A to Z by author. They describe the chosen books as concisely as possible (while aiming to avoid too many 'spoilers') and say something briefly about the writer and his or her life and career. Significant film versions of the books (with dates of release) are noted where applicable, followed by *Read on* lists comprising books by the same author, books by stylistically similar writers or books on a theme relevant to the main entry. Scattered throughout the text there are also *Read on a Theme* menus which list between six and a dozen titles united by a common theme. These *Read on a Theme* lists also include only titles which have won some kind of prize. The *Read on* lists at the end of an author entry do include some titles which have remained unrewarded, although they are all, I hope, worth reading. The symbol ❯❯ before an author name indicates that the author is one of those covered in the A to Z entries.

Other books in this series cover crime fiction, science fiction and fantasy fiction and, for that reason, I have not included any novels in the main entries in this volume which have won prizes specifically related to those genres. I would have been happy to include more winners of prizes for fiction in languages other than English but too often in my research I discovered that these winners had either never been translated into English or, if they had, they had been allowed to slip out of print.

INTRODUCTION

Literary prizes have been with us for a long time. There is an argument for saying that, as with so many aspects of human endeavour, the ancient Greeks got there first. What were the regular contests in which Greek poets declaimed their verse and competed for accolades but a type of literary prizegiving? Galloping swiftly through two millennia and more of history, it was in the nineteenth century that the literary prize arrived in something like a form we would recognise today. The wealthy patron was a creature of the past and writers were now only too happy to strive for the financial incentives that newspapers and magazines held out in the shape of monetary awards and competitions. Some survived almost exclusively on the money they won. Edgar Allan Poe, for instance, when he had no steadier source of income, made a living (although not much of one) out of prizes awarded by publications like the *Baltimore Saturday Visiter* and the *Southern Literary Messenger* for poems and short stories.

However, the modern era for literary prizes began with the grand-daddy of all such awards – the Nobel Prize. The inventor of dynamite, Alfred Nobel, died in 1896. Perhaps eager to make amends for a life spent creating weapons of death and destruction, Nobel left huge sums of money for the establishment of a series of prizes in different areas, including literature. The Nobel Prize in Literature was first awarded in

1901 to the now largely forgotten French poet René Sully-Prudhomme. Other prizes followed in the next twenty years – the Prix Goncourt and the Prix Femina in France in 1903 and 1905, the Pulitzer Prizes in the USA in 1917. The first major prize in Britain which still survives, the James Tait Black Memorial Prize, was instituted in 1919. The first winner was Hugh Walpole, not now a name that would be at the top of anybody's list of great writers of the period, but the winners of the James Tait Black in its first decade did include the likes of D.H. Lawrence, Arnold Bennett and E.M. Forster.

Since the Second World War, and more especially in the last thirty years, there has been an explosion in the numbers of literary prizes awarded. The Booker (now Man Booker) Prize began in the late 1960s and, although it failed to ignite much enthusiasm in its early years, the decision to televise the awards ceremony in 1981, combined with a run of exciting and interesting winners, turned it into the institution it now is. The prize money – now a whopping £50,000 – helped to make it popular with the writers who won it if no one else. So did the increase in sales that winning the Booker could now guarantee. A work of literary fiction that would normally sell fewer than two thousand copies might now easily multiply its sales by a factor of one hundred or more. In Britain, the Booker was followed by the Whitbread (now the Costa) Awards in 1971 and, in the 1990s, by the Orange. Other prizes, smaller in terms of money and publicity, continued to proliferate. By the dawn of the new millennium, there were so many literary prizes that there were handbooks produced just to list them all for weary booksellers and librarians.

All of this begs the difficult questions. Apart from the lucky winners, who do they benefit? What use are literary prizes? Certainly they are not always handed out to those writers whom posterity later judges to have been most deserving. As critics of the big prizes have often pointed out in the past, judging panels often get it wrong. Take the Nobel as a prime example. Who now has heard of Henrik Pontoppidan or Erik Axel Karlfeldt? Of Frans Eemil Sillanpää or Yasunari Kawabata? Yet all four men won the Nobel Prize in Literature. Which is more than can be said for Joseph Conrad, Henry James, Marcel Proust, F. Scott Fitzgerald, Virginia Woolf and Graham Greene who were all nominated for the Prize but failed to come up to the exacting standards of the committee of the Swedish Academy which hands it out. Look back at the list of winners of the Pulitzer Prize for Fiction (or the Pulitzer Prize for the Novel as it was until 1948). *The Able McLaughlins* by Margaret Wilson, *The Store* by Thomas Sigismund Stribling and *Journey in the Dark* by Martin Flavin probably don't ring too many bells today.

However, the incompetence of judging panels in the past can be exaggerated. It's a difficult job they undertake. No one has a crystal ball in which they can witness the changing of public taste and the waxing and waning of authorial reputations in the years to come. And many of the decisions that judges made years ago don't seem too bad today. The Nobel committee has undoubtedly made some howlers in days gone by but they have also picked Thomas Mann, Andre Gidé, William Faulkner, Samuel Beckett and Saul Bellow. They have often enough made the right call. The same is true of the Pulitzer. Surely no one would dispute that Steinbeck's *The Grapes of Wrath*, Harper Lee's *To Kill a Mockingbird*, John Kennedy Toole's *A Confederacy of Dunces* and Alice Walker's *The Color Purple* are all significant works of American literature. And they all won the Pulitzer.

If nothing else, prizes offer a path through the literary labyrinth. In a publishing world where thousands of novels arrive on the bookshop shelves every year, readers need some means of choosing what to buy and what to read. This book is based on the premise that reading books that have won the major prizes is a good way of sampling the vast range of contemporary literary fiction that is available. Not all prize-winners are necessarily worth reading. But I believe that the one hundred books I have chosen for this brief guide all are.

A–ZOFENTRIES

PETER ACKROYD (b. 1949) UK

HAWKSMOOR (1985)

Guardian Fiction Prize 1985

Much of Peter Ackroyd's very varied work – and he has produced fiction, biographies, poetry, history and criticism in his career – is linked by two preoccupations. One is his fascination with London, the city of his birth. The other is his belief in the intimate connections between past and present. Both these preoccupations are certainly on display in his fiction which includes a story set in the world of the Victorian music-hall (*Dan Leno and the Limehouse Golem*), the tale of a man who inherits a house in Clerkenwell once owned by a famous Elizabethan magician (*The House of Doctor Dee*) and a novel which reworks the lives of the London essayist Charles Lamb and his sister (*The Lambs of London*). *Hawksmoor*, which won both the Guardian Fiction Prize and the Whitbread Award in the year of its publication, is usually considered his most powerful and original novel. In this dazzlingly inventive and cleverly written book, a contemporary detective (possessed of the same name as the eighteenth-century architect Nicholas Hawksmoor) moves towards a mystical encounter with forces from the past as he investigates a series of murders in London churches. History reaches out to seize the detective in the shape of Nicholas Dyer, an early eighteenth-century Satanist who, just to add an extra ingredient to Ackroyd's already complicated mix, shares many of the characteristics of the real, historical Nicholas Hawksmoor. Dyer is a man in revolt against the emerging rationalism of his age, believing, in his own words, that 'there is no light without darknesse and no substance without shaddowe'. The churches he designs conceal terrible secrets which echo down the ages and effect the crimes which Hawksmoor the detective investigates in the twentieth century. Written in part in a brilliantly reconstructed version of eighteenth-century prose, Ackroyd's novel is an exhilarating narrative in which two eras meet and intertwine.

🕮 Read on

Chatterton; *The House of Doctor Dee*

John Banville, *Doctor Copernicus*; ›› Iain Sinclair, *White Chappell, Scarlet Tracings*

CHIMAMANDA NGOZI ADICHIE (b. 1977)

NIGERIA

HALF OF A YELLOW SUN (2006)

Orange Prize 2007

Chimamanda Ngozi Adichie, born in Nigeria and educated there and in the United States, won the Orange Prize with what was only her second book. She had nearly done so with her first (*Purple Hibiscus*), the story of a fifteen-year-old Nigerian girl who leaves her privileged but religiously repressive family life behind her when her father is obliged to send her away to live with her aunt, which was shortlisted for the prestigious, women-only prize. *Half of a Yellow Sun*, the novel with which she took the award, is a powerful story set amidst the horrors and upheaval of the civil war in Nigeria in the 1960s and takes its title from the design of the flag of the short-lived Biafran nation. The brutal and bloody events of the war are seen through the eyes of a group of vividly realised characters as they find themselves swept up by historical forces beyond their control. Ugwu is a teenager employed as a houseboy by Odenigbo, a charismatic university professor, who is fired by revolutionary and anti-colonial zeal. Olanna is the beautiful and well-educated Igbo woman who has abandoned her life in the capital Lagos in order to be with Odenigbo. Olanna's twin sister Kainene is involved with an Englishman who is living in Nigeria while he researches a book about the country's tribal art. As Nigerian forces advance, all of them, forced to flee for their lives, find their beliefs and their emotional attachments tested to the limits and beyond. Adichie, a young writer recreating events which her parents' generation endured, has produced a novel of exceptional depth and quality. As the elder statesman of African literature, Chinua Achebe, has remarked, 'We do not usually associate wisdom with beginners but here is a new writer endowed with the gift of ancient storytellers.'

🐚 Read on

Purple Hibiscus; *The Thing Around Your Neck* (short stories)

Chinua Achebe, *Things Fall Apart*; Petina Gappah, *An Elegy for Easterly*; Helen Oyeyemi, *The Icarus Girl*

ARAVIND ADIGA (b. 1974) INDIA

THE WHITE TIGER (2008)

Man Booker Prize 2008

In a series of letters addressed to Wen Jiabao, the Prime Minister of China who is about to pay a state visit to India, Balram Halwai, the anti-hero of first-time novelist Aravind Adiga's savagely satirical book, takes it upon himself to introduce the Chinese visitor to some of the realities of the country. 'In the belief that the future of the world lies with the yellow man and the brown man now that our erstwhile master, the white-skinned man, has wasted himself through buggery, mobile phone usage and drug abuse,' Balram sets about educating the premier in the way the new India works. He does this by relating his own story. He is currently, as he is eager to point out, a successful businessman and entrepreneur in the up-and-coming city of Bangalore but this was not always the case. Balram was the son of a rickshaw-puller and hailed from 'the Darkness', his name for the vast areas of the sub-continent still mired in poverty. He describes with the precision of an insider the petty indignities and humiliations of being poor and a servant to others. And he confesses just what he has been prepared to do to escape them. Balram was once driver to Mr. Ashok, wealthy scion of a landowning family, but an act of violence has freed him from his servitude and set him on the path to the prosperity he now enjoys. Deprivation creates monsters among the deprived and Balram reveals the events that turned him into one of them. Written in its narrator's unforgettable voice – witty, unblinkered, direct and, in the last analysis, utterly amoral – *The White Tiger* is a book that provides a new perspective on the extremes of Indian life as the country races to become one of the world's great economies. It's a book that throws a terrible light on 'the Darkness' and the creatures it produces.

📖 Read on
Between the Assassinations
Mohammed Hanif, *A Case of Exploding Mangoes*; Vikas Swarup, *Q & A*

KATE ATKINSON (b. 1951) UK

BEHIND THE SCENES AT THE MUSEUM (1995)

Whitbread Book of the Year 1995

Born in York in 1951, Kate Atkinson only began to publish her fiction in the 1990s but she immediately showed an originality and individual style that marked her out as a significant talent. *Behind the Scenes at the Museum* was her first novel and it won the Whitbread Book of the Year award. Set in the 1950s and 1960s, it is the story of Ruby Lennox, growing up in the family home above a pet shop in the shadow of York Minster. Opening, like a kind of welfare state *Tristram Shandy*, with the moment of Ruby's conception, heralded by a few grunts and groans from her father while her mother feigns sleep, this is a family saga with a difference. Told in the funny and quirky voice of its central character, it darts back and forth in time. Interwoven with Ruby's story (in a series of footnotes) are those of her great-grandmother, her grandmother, uncles, aunts and cousins as they struggle through two world wars. But there are small gaps in the narrative, hints of something amiss. Family secrets, long hidden, begin to surface – one so devastating that it overwhelms Ruby even as it explains so much that has been puzzling in her life. Atkinson finally ties together all the loose ends of her meandering tale and illuminates the meanings of the hints, clues and allusions she has strewn through the text. In the years since the publication of *Behind the Scenes at the Museum*, Kate Atkinson has written half-a-dozen other novels including *Human Croquet*, the extravagantly told story of a family whose glory days are in the past, and several offbeat but engaging works of crime fiction featuring an Edinburgh private investigator named Jackson Brodie. All of them have embodied the same darkly comic sensibility that pervaded *Behind the Scenes at the Museum* but there is a case to be made that her debut novel remains her most characteristic.

⮒ Read on

Human Croquet; *Case Histories* (the first of the Jackson Brodie books) Liz Jensen, *The Ninth Life of Louis Drax*; Maggie O'Farrell, *The Vanishing Act of Esme Lennox*

MARGARET ATWOOD (b. 1939) CANADA

THE BLIND ASSASSIN (2000)

Booker Prize 2000

Poet and short story-writer as well as novelist, Margaret Atwood is one of the most gifted of contemporary writers and her fiction has ranged from the dazzling SF dystopias of *The Handmaid's Tale* and *Oryx and Crake* to *Alias Grace*, an exploration of women's sexuality and social roles wrapped up in a gripping and enigmatic story of a nineteenth-century housemaid who may or may not have been a murderess. Her novels have won many prizes in her native Canada and she has been shortlisted five times for the Man Booker Prize, going on to win it in 2000 with *The Blind Assassin*. In this remarkable novel an elderly woman attempts to understand the secret history of her family and to unravel the enigma of her sister's death many decades before. The book opens with the simple, declarative words of the octogenarian Iris Chase Griffen: 'Ten days after the war ended, my sister Laura drove a car off a bridge.' It continues with Iris looking back on the lives she and her sister led in the 1920s and the 1930s and the events and relationships that shaped them. Interwoven with Iris's account are extracts from a novel, entitled *The Blind Assassin*, which was published after Laura's death as her posthumous work and became a cult success. This novel seems to be a *roman à clef* in which the story of Laura's romance with a radical agitator is hidden beneath a thin veneer of fiction. Within the novel within a novel another story emerges when the two lovers invent a pulp fantasy adventure which echoes their own lives. As the different narratives intertwine, Margaret Atwood gradually leads her readers towards a startling revelation which overturns all assumptions they may have made about the relationship between the 'truth' of her memoir and the 'fiction' of her sister's novel.

🕮 Read on

Alias Grace; *Oryx and Crake*; *The Robber Bride*
Alison Lurie, *Imaginary Friends*; ➤ Carol Shields, *The Stone Diaries*

BERYL BAINBRIDGE (b. 1932) UK

MASTER GEORGIE (1998)

W.H. Smith Literary Award 1999

In her earlier career Beryl Bainbridge wrote novels that ranged from the story of two Liverpudlian women on a works outing interrupted by death and black farce (*The Bottle Factory Outing*) to a laconic tale which takes as its starting point the possibility that Hitler spent a brief period in Liverpool before the First World War (*Young Adolf*). Her fiction in the last twenty years has been all set in the past. *The Birthday Boys* took a sidelong look at the legendary heroics of Captain Scott and his men; *Every Man for Himself* is set on the Titanic during its first and fatal voyage. Of these historical novels the most memorable is probably *Master Georgie* which was shortlisted for the Booker Prize as well as winning a number of other awards. The novel takes place in the 1850s during the Crimean War but this is not the familiar war of Florence Nightingale and the Charge of the Light Brigade. Bainbridge focuses not on grand events and famous people but on the smaller scale, individual tragedies of her characters. George Hardy is a prosperous surgeon and enthusiast for the new art of photography who volunteers his medical services to the war effort. Accompanying him to the Crimea are his adoring adopted sister, Myrtle, his brother-in-law Dr Potter and an ex-street urchin called Pompey Jones who has a mysterious hold over Georgie. Structured around the notion of six photographic plates, *Master Georgie* chronicles the party's disintegration in the face of the death and disease they find in the Crimea and the gradual emergence of hidden truths about their personal and erotic entanglements. Told in a variety of narrative voices, including those of Myrtle and Dr. Potter, the novel is a dark, disturbing and moving tale that lingers long in the memory after reading.

📖 Read on

An Awfully Big Adventure (set in a shabby provincial theatre in the 1950s); *The Birthday Boys*; *Every Man for Himself*
Penelope Fitzgerald, *The Gate of Angels*; ➤➤ Hilary Mantel, *Beyond Black*; Matthew Plampin, *The Street Philosopher*

J.G. BALLARD (1930–2009) UK

EMPIRE OF THE SUN (1984)

Guardian Fiction Prize 1984

When J.G. Ballard first began to publish his fiction in the late 1950s and early 1960s he was immediately classified as a science fiction writer. Novels such as *The Drowned World*, set in a post-apocalyptic London, certainly seemed to suggest that this was the best way to pigeonhole him but his works of the 1970s (*Crash*, *Concrete Island*, *High Rise*) revealed him looking for his subjects more in the urban landscape of contemporary society than in the future worlds of SF. His 1984 novel *Empire of the Sun* saw him turning his back on both the present and the future and looking to the past for inspiration. In this extraordinary and compelling novel about one boy's life in the internment camps of Japanese-occupied Shanghai during the Second World War, Ballard reworks the events of his own traumatic childhood. Like his young hero Jim Graham, Ballard was a boy living in Shanghai's International Settlement as the clouds of war gathered. The novel opens on what Franklin Roosevelt called the 'date which will live in infamy' – December 7th 1941, the day not only of Pearl Harbor but also of an attack on British and American warships docked at Shanghai. In the chaos that follows, Jim is separated from his parents and forced to fend for himself. He ends up in one of the camps that the swiftly victorious Japanese establish and, thrust into a new world where human beings shed the accretions of civilisation in order to survive, he loses his innocence about human nature. In the last twenty-five years of his life, Ballard published some remarkable novels (*Cocaine Nights*, *Super-Cannes*) which straddle the gap between social analysis and the prediction of future social developments but many would argue that his best book remained *Empire of the Sun* – one of the most compelling coming-of-age stories in twentieth-century fiction.

🎞 **Film version:** *Empire of the Sun* (1987, directed by Steven Spielberg and starring Christian Bale as Jim Graham)

📚 **Read on**
The Kindness of Women (a sequel to *Empire of the Sun* which follows Jim Graham from Shanghai to England and into later life); *Cocaine Nights*; *Super-Cannes*
➤➤ John Lanchester, *Fragrant Harbour*

NICOLA BARKER (b. 1966) UK

DARKMANS (2007)

Hawthornden Prize 2008

Nicola Barker's novels and stories, unmistakably offbeat and quirky, are unlike those of almost any other contemporary novelist. Usually set in some of the least glamorous and scenically attractive areas of contemporary Britain – Palmers Green, the Isle of Sheppey, Canvey Island – her books present a contrast between the mundane, if indefinably sinister, topography and the oddballs who people it. Her characters are those who, through choice or fate, fail to fit in to society. They are all weirdly memorable, as is Barker's elaborate prose style which is rich in darkly comic metaphor and simile and packed with punning playfulness. *Darkmans* is her most ambitious novel so far and takes place in early twenty-first century Ashford which, with its ring roads and service stations and soulless housing estates, is the unlikely stage on which a malevolently mischievous jester from the past threatens to make an unscheduled reappearance. As the other characters – Beede and his estranged, drug-dealing son Kane, Kane's former girlfriend, the foul-mouthed Kelly, a Kurdish repairman named Gaffar, a dazed and possibly narcoleptic German named Dory and many others – go about their ordinary business, the figure of John Scogin, jester at the court of Edward IV and subject of historical research by the elder Beede, sniggers in the background. Beede feels Scogin's presence in his own body; Dory unwittingly recreates some of the jester's most cruelly comic pranks; Dory's precocious son Fleet, who has been building a matchstick model of a cathedral in France, refers to his father as 'John'. History is still haunting the dismally modern streets of Ashford and, in the shape of Scogin, is lurking in the shadows to mug the town's inhabitants. *Darkmans* is an endlessly inventive and very funny book. It brilliantly embodies what one critic has described as Barker's 'determinedly perverse and ungovernable imagination'.

≋ Read on

Wide Open (earlier novel which won the International IMPAC Dublin Literary Award); *Behindlings*

Catherine O'Flynn, *What Was Lost*; Ali Smith, *The Accidental*

JULIAN BARNES (b. 1946) UK

FLAUBERT'S PARROT (1984)

Geoffrey Faber Memorial Prize 1985

Julian Barnes worked as a lexicographer on the Oxford English Dictionary before moving into journalism as a reviewer, literary editor and TV critic, and he published his first novel, *Metroland*, in 1980. In the thirty years since his debut he has written nine further novels and published several volumes of short stories and essays. His most recent novel is *Arthur and George* which takes a real story involving Sir Arthur Conan Doyle, the creator of Sherlock Holmes, and his attempts to win justice for a wrongly imprisoned solicitor, and creates an elegant narrative about two very different men whose lives accidentally intertwine. It was much acclaimed on publication and was shortlisted for the Man Booker Prize. Barnes had been shortlisted for the award twice before, once for *England, England*, a clever and often very funny satire of ideas of Englishness, and once for *Flaubert's Parrot*. This last book was his third work of fiction under his own name (he had also published crime fiction under the pseudonym of Dan Kavanagh) and, as well as being shortlisted for the Booker, it won the Geoffrey Faber Memorial Prize and the Prix Médicis in France. Its narrator is a doctor, Geoffrey Braithwaite, who is obsessively interested in the nineteenth-century French author of *Madame Bovary*. Fascinated not just by the novels but by the minutiae of Flaubert's life and the interaction between the biographical and the fictional, Braithwaite tries to establish the truth about one minor, peripheral detail of his hero's writing life – the fate of a stuffed parrot which had once sat on the writer's desk. A crude description of the book might make it sound dry and uninteresting to all except scholars of nineteenth century French literature but, as Barnes unfolds the story of Braithwaite's obsession, *Flaubert's Parrot* becomes a witty and sophisticated examination of what we make of the past and how fiction, biography and history interpret it.

🥢 Read on

A History of the World in 10½ Chapters; *Arthur and George*
>> A.S. Byatt, *Possession*; Gustave Flaubert, *Madame Bovary*; Vladimir Nabokov, *Pale Fire*

SEBASTIAN BARRY (b. 1955) IRELAND

THE SECRET SCRIPTURE (2008)

Costa Book of the Year 2008

A playwright and poet as well as a novelist, Sebastian Barry is one of the most original and powerful Irish writers of his generation. His earlier novel, *A Long, Long Way*, about a Dubliner fighting in the First World War, was shortlisted for the Man Booker Prize as was *The Secret Scripture* but neither book went on to win. However, *The Secret Scripture* did take the Costa Book of the Year award in the year it was published. Its story is told in two narrative voices. The first is that of Roseanne McNulty, an elderly woman, possibly a centenarian (although she cannot be sure), who lives a forgotten life in the decrepit mental hospital in Roscommon which has been her home for many decades. Struggling to organise her memories of her sad and damaged life, and to recall the reasons for her incarceration in the asylum, she embarks on the writing of a 'Testimony of Herself'. The second narrator in Barry's novel is Dr. Grene, a psychiatrist in the hospital grieving over the death of his wife, who attempts to unravel the mysteries of Roseanne's life himself. As Roseanne unfolds her possibly unreliable story of growing up in Sligo during the years immediately after the Irish Civil War and of the terrible combination of misogyny and petty local politics which resulted in her being branded as insane, Grene delves deeper and deeper into the surviving records of her case. What he finds in the course of his investigation is a secret that not only changes his ideas about Roseanne but unsettles his own sense of who he is. *The Secret Scripture* is a remarkable novel, a beautifully written account of a lost and thwarted life which casts an unforgiving light on some of the darker truths of Ireland's twentieth-century history.

📖 Read on

A Long, Long Way; *The Whereabouts of Eneas McNulty*
>> Seamus Deane, *Reading in the Dark*; Anne Enright, *The Gathering*

RONAN BENNETT (b. 1956) UK

HAVOC IN ITS THIRD YEAR (2004)

Hughes and Hughes Irish Novel of the Year 2005

Ronan Bennett was born in Belfast and, as a teenage Republican activist in the city, was wrongfully convicted of murder. He spent eighteen months in the notorious Long Kesh prison before his conviction was overturned and he was released. In London in the late 1970s, he was again in prison, accused of conspiracy to cause explosions, before he was acquitted of the charge at an Old Bailey trial. He went on to study history at King's College, London and to complete a doctorate on crime and punishment in seventeenth-century England, undertaking research on which he was able to draw when writing *Havoc in its Third Year*. This was his fourth novel and followed a critical success with *The Catastrophist*, a political thriller set in the Belgian Congo in the years just before it received its independence which had been shortlisted for the Whitbread Novel Award. *Havoc in its Third Year* is set in a small northern English town in the 1630s. Its central character,

John Brigge, is the coroner for the district. Newly a father, and driven by a revitalised passion for his wife, he would prefer to ignore the internecine power struggles of the town's elite, but the case of an Irishwoman accused of infanticide nags at his conscience. The great men of the town want to hang her, but Brigge refuses to hasten the woman's death and suspects that there is much more to the case than is first apparent. In pursuing it, he sets out on a path that threatens to lead to his own destruction. Bennett's gripping novel may be a work of historical fiction but, like all of his books, it is driven by political passion. On one level, it may be about Puritanism in action in the seventeenth century but it also explores questions of injustice and intolerance that are still very much alive today.

⮳ Read on

The Catastrophist; *Zugzwang*

Geraldine Brooks, *Year of Wonders*; Maria McCann, *As Meat Loves Salt*

WILLIAM BOYD (b. 1952) UK

A GOOD MAN IN AFRICA (1981)

Somerset Maugham Award 1981

In the course of a thirty-year writing career, William Boyd has published volumes of short stories, a fat collection of reviews and essays, a spoof biography of an invented artist and ten novels. From *An Ice-Cream War*, set against the backdrop of the forgotten African campaigns of the First

World War, through *The New Confessions*, the fictional memoirs of a failed film-maker obsessed by the idea of making a nine-hour epic based on Rousseau's *Confessions*, to *Restless*, Costa Novel of the Year in 2009, his fiction has won plaudits and been shortlisted for major prizes. This has been the case since his very first novel, *A Good Man in Africa*, was published in 1981. Not only did it win the Somerset Maugham Award it also took the Whitbread First Novel Award in that year The anti-hero of Boyd's satire of the last, limp flourishes of colonialism, Morgan Leafy, is the First Secretary of the British Deputy Commission in the imaginary West African country of Kinjanja. Slobbish, resentful and frustrated in his career and in his pursuit of his boss's daughter, Morgan is a man profoundly disillusioned with life and most of what it has to offer. Only beer and sex provide any comfort. 'They were the only things in his life that didn't consistently let him down,' he muses at one point in the book. 'They sometimes did, but not in the randomly cruel and arbitrary way that the other features of the world conspired to confuse and frustrate him.' As Morgan battles with local politics and politicians, his own desires and the humiliations fate throws at him, he becomes, like other anti-heroes of British comic fiction, a curiously likeable and vulnerable character. With echoes not only of Evelyn Waugh but also Graham Greene, *A Good Man in Africa* is very funny but there is a sadness lurking not far beneath the comic surface.

🐦 Read on

An Ice-Cream War; *The New Confessions*; *Restless*
Martin Amis, *The Information*; Evelyn Waugh, *Decline and Fall*

A.S. BYATT (b. 1936) UK

POSSESSION (1990)

Booker Prize 1990

For more than forty years, A.S. Byatt has been publishing generous and erudite fiction, informed by her own expressed desire to write about 'the life of the mind as well as of society and the relations between people'. The most successful novel of her career, and the one which won the Booker Prize in 1990, is *Possession*, a dazzlingly clever narrative which moves back and forth between past and present. In it, Byatt unravels the interlocking lives of two contemporary literary researchers who are themselves delving into the biographies of two Victorian poets, Randolph Henry Ash and Christabel LaMotte. It has long been assumed that Ash was a doting and faithful husband and that LaMotte's emotional commitment was to her own sex but the two academics, Roland Mitchell and Maud Bailey, gradually unearth evidence that suggests a different story. They discover that the nineteenth-century writers shared an illicit but all-consuming passion and, as they do so, they themselves stretch the emotional bonds they have placed upon their lives. The more they pursue the ghosts of Ash and LaMotte's passion, the more they get in touch with their own feelings. They are people who have been shaped but also shackled by their devotion to literature and intellectual pursuits but, in this instance at least, their researches enable them to cast aside some of their chains. The book is daring in the material it uses to tell its story. It includes lengthy examples of Ash's and LaMotte's poetry (based on the work of Browning and Christina Rossetti, they demonstrate Byatt's remarkable gifts as a literary ventriloquist), as well as letters and other documents that the two contemporary researchers investigate. It is through the hints and clues contained in these texts that the narrative – a compelling hybrid of detective story, romance and historical novel – largely emerges.

🕮 Read on

The Biographer's Tale; *The Children's Book*; *The Virgin in the Garden*
>> Peter Carey, *Oscar and Lucinda*; Iris Murdoch, *The Sea, the Sea*

PETER CAREY (b. 1943) AUSTRALIA
TRUE HISTORY OF THE KELLY GANG (2000)
Booker Prize 2001

Peter Carey first came to notice as a short-story writer in the 1970s. In the following decade he published two big, ambitious novels which combined stories of the Australian past with elements of the fantastic and the surreal. *Illywhacker* is the tale of an ancient and outrageous liar inventing a life story in which he seems to have personally supervised the entire history of white people in Australia; in *Oscar and Lucinda* two nineteenth-century dreamers and gamblers join forces to transport a great glass church into the outback. Carey seems comfortable when he is reinventing the nineteenth century in his fiction. *Jack Maggs* is a book that skilfully mingles events copied from Charles Dickens's life with a reworking of the plot of *Great Expectations* to create a new narrative. And in *True History of the Kelly Gang*, Carey chooses to tackle the great Australian story, both 'true' and legendary, of the bushwhacker Ned Kelly. Told by the semi-literate Kelly himself, the book takes the form of a series of manuscripts supposedly written by him for his daughter to read after his death. 'I lost my own father at 12 yr. of age and know what it is to be raised on lies and silences,' the first of these haphazardly punctuated texts begins, 'my dear daughter you are presently too young to understand a word I write but this history is for you and will contain no single lie may I burn in Hell if I speak false.' The truths that Kelly tries to tell his daughter record the poverty and persecution that drive him into crime, his formation of the notorious Kelly Gang, his love for her mother and the final, climactic confrontation between his gang and the police in the small town of Glenrowan. The voice that Carey creates for his bushranging anti-hero is so extraordinarily vivid and brings the legendary figure to life with such immediacy that it is little surprise that the book won the Booker Prize for its author for the second time.

🕮 Read on

Illywhacker; *Oscar and Lucinda* (Carey's first Booker winner); *Jack Maggs*

Robert Drewe, *Our Sunshine* (another Australian novelist tells Kelly's story); ›› David Malouf, *The Conversations at Curlow Creek*

READONATHEME: AUSTRALIA

Murray Bail, *Eucalyptus* (Australian Literature Society Gold Medal 1999)

Richard Flanagan, *Gould's Book of Fish* (Commonwealth Writers' Prize 2002)

David Foster, *The Glade Within the Grove* (Miles Franklin Award 1997)

Michelle de Kretser, *The Lost Dog* (Australian Literature Society Gold Medal 2008)

Rodney Hall, *The Day We Had Hitler Home* (Australian Literature Society Gold Medal 2001)

Elizabeth Jolley, *The Well* (Miles Franklin Award 1986)

➤➤ David Malouf, *The Great World* (Commonwealth Writers' Prize 1991)

Roger McDonald, *The Ballad of Desmond Kale* (Miles Franklin Award 2006)

Randolph Stow, *To the Islands* (Miles Franklin Award 1958)

Alexis Wright, *Carpentaria* (Miles Franklin Award 2007)

ANGELA CARTER (1940–92) UK

NIGHTS AT THE CIRCUS (1984)

James Tait Black Memorial Prize 1984

Angela Carter was one of the most imaginative British writers of the past fifty years and her early death was a tremendous loss to literature. Her varied inspiration included fairytales, Jung's theory of the collective unconscious, horror movies and the fantasies of such writers as Edgar Allan Poe and Mary Shelley. Her early books range from Gothic reworkings of fairytales (*The Bloody Chamber*) to such dystopian nightmares as *The Passion of New Eve*, set in a near-future USA where a young man, Evelyn hides in the California desert, only to be kid-napped by devotees of the multi-breasted, all-engulfing Earth Mother, who rapes him, castrates him and remakes him as a woman, Eve. Later novels mix history and fantasy in giving full rein to Carter's gifts for the baroquely imagined, the theatrical and the picaresque. In *Nights at the Circus*, for example, a reporter named Walser is investigating the claims of Fevvers, a winged trapeze artiste who may or may not be an angel disguised as a blowsy, turn-of-the-century circus *aerialiste*. Walser is intent on kickstarting his journalistic career by revealing Fevvers as a fraud but he is unable to do so and ends instead by falling in love with her. Fevvers tells the reporter of her early life in a brothel, the object of strange and violent male lusts, and reveals her escape into freak shows and the circus which grant her fame and a new freedom. The story continues as she and Walser, now a member of Colonel Kearney's magic, surreal circus himself, tour Russia. As a train takes the circus across Siberia, it crashes and Fevvers and Walser are separated, each to endure their own purgatorial journey in the wilderness before they are reunited at the novel's end. Filled with wonder and surreal invention, *Nights at the Circus* is one of the most vividly readable and original books of the 1980s.

🕮 Read on
The Magic Toyshop; *Wise Children*
>> Jeanette Winterson, *Sexing the Cherry*

BRUCE CHATWIN (1940–89) UK

ON THE BLACK HILL (1982)

James Tait Black Memorial Prize 1982

Bruce Chatwin was an author who spent his career ignoring the often artificial barriers erected between one form of writing and another. In his 1977 book *In Patagonia*, winner of the Hawthornden Prize, fact and fiction, anecdote and information, past and present all combine to produce an utterly unique account of a voyage to the foot of South America. *The Songlines*, published in 1986, is billed as a novel but it includes a character named Bruce Chatwin and the border between fiction and travel memoir in it often seems difficult to fix. *On the Black Hill* is a more conventional novel – the story of identical twin brothers, who spend their entire lives on a remote Welsh farm. Neither of them marries; they seem sufficient unto themselves. 'For forty-two years,' the book begins, 'Lewis and Benjamin Jones slept side by side, in their parents' bed, at their farm which was known as "The Vision".' Unlike the nomadic peoples who fascinated Chatwin and who appeared in books like *The Songlines*, Lewis and Benjamin go nowhere. Their lives are defined by the few square miles of Welsh countryside in which they are rooted and the tumultuous events of the twentieth century only distantly touch them. Much that happens elsewhere seems remote and almost unreal to them. When the First World War begins, somewhere over the horizon, they refuse to fight in it – not because of any deep-rooted pacifism but because they cannot see that it has any connection with them. They are attuned only to the rhythms of the small world into which they have been born. As Chatwin focuses ever more closely on the small details of the seemingly humdrum and uneventful lives of the twins, his book develops into a moving and beautifully written meditation on isolation and the interaction between landscape and personality.

🎬 **Film version:** *On the Black Hill* (1987)

📗 **Read on**
In Patagonia; *The Songlines*; *Utz*
Peter Ho Davies, *The Welsh Girl*; F.M. Mayor, *The Rector's Daughter* (for a very different writer's tale of loneliness and isolation)

JONATHAN COE (b. 1961) UK

WHAT A CARVE UP! (1994)

John Llewellyn Rhys Prize 1994

Jonathan Coe had already written three novels which had gathered critical praise but limited sales when he made a break-through to a larger readership with *What a Carve Up!* Taking its name from a 1962 horror-comedy movie, this is a deliciously unforgiving satire of the rampant materialism of the 1980s, focusing on one family – the spectacularly unlovely Winshaws. Different members of the clan – an arms dealer selling weapons to Saddam Hussein, a banker with a finger in every financially fishy pie, a journalist with no moral scruples whatsoever – represent, individually and collectively, all that was wrong about the country in that low, dishonest decade. Reclusive novelist Michael Owen is commissioned to write a family biography and his growing conviction that the Winshaws have ruined his life persuades him to take his revenge upon them by acting out the film with which he is obsessed, murdering each member of the family in a way that makes the punishment fit the crime. Along the way the story of each member of the Winshaw family unfolds and his or her part in the ruin of the nation is revealed. Since his success with *What a Carve Up!* Coe has published five other novels, most notably *The Rotters' Club*, in which 1970s Britain – its music, fashion and political tensions – is filtered through the experiences of four Birmingham schoolboys trying to impose their own developing personalities on the world, and its sequel, *The Closed Circle*, which returns to the same characters as they approach middle age. He has shown himself to be an adventurous and original writer with an eye for exploring the possibilities of the novel as a literary form (it is no great surprise that he is also the biographer of B.S. Johnson, the restlessly experimental novelist of the 1960s) but he is also one of the funniest and most perceptive of contemporary authors.

🕮 Read on

The Rotters' Club; *The Closed Circle*; *The Rain Before It Falls*
>> William Boyd, *Armadillo*; >> Alan Hollinghurst, *The Line of Beauty*

J.M. COETZEE (b. 1940) SOUTH AFRICA

DISGRACE (1999)

Booker Prize 1999

J.M. Coetzee won the Nobel Prize for Literature in 2003 and is one of only two writers to have won the Booker Prize twice. He has published more than a dozen novels in the decades since the appearance of his first, *Dusklands*, in the early 1970s and these have ranged from a re-working of the Robinson Crusoe story in which a woman joins the two castaways from Defoe's original book (*Foe*) to a story which focuses on the nineteenth-century Russian author Dostoevsky during a period of crisis (*The Master of Petersburg*). However, most of his fiction has wrestled with the problems and the pains of his native land, South Africa. His first Booker success came with his 1983 novel *Life and Times of Michael K*, in which the title character, a simple-minded gardener, struggles to retain his dignity and worth whilst the country is torn apart by civil war. The central character of *Disgrace*, the second of Coetzee's novels to win the Booker, is David Lurie, a middle-aged university professor. Lurie has twice failed in marriage and he seduces his young female students with cynical regularity, while still proclaiming his faith in the 'romance' that fuelled the romantic poets he loves. After one particularly joyless sexual encounter – very nearly a rape – the student complains to the university authorities and Lurie, asked to apologise, instead resigns. Largely unrepentant, he goes to stay with his daughter on her farm in a remote part of South Africa. There he and his daughter, striving to come to some sense of accommodation with one another, are the victims of a brutal attack that changes them both. *Disgrace* is a daring novel – daring in creating an unsympathetic narrator, daring in its willingness to tackle sensitive issues of gender and race, and daring in presenting an unflinchingly pessimistic view of the effect political change can have on personal relationships.

🐱 Read on

Elizabeth Costello; *Age of Iron*

Andre Brink, *A Dry White Season*; Nadine Gordimer, *The Conservationist*

READONATHEME: NOVELS BY NOBEL PRIZE WINNERS

The Nobel Prize for Literature is given for a body of work rather than for an individual work but the following is a list of selected novels by writers who have won the prize

Saul Bellow (Nobel Laureate 1976), *Herzog*
Albert Camus (Nobel Laureate 1957), *The Outsider*
William Golding (Nobel Laureate 1983), *Lord of the Flies*
Günter Grass (Nobel Laureate 1999), *The Tin Drum*
Knut Hamsun (Nobel Laureate 1920), *Growth of the Soil*
Hermann Hesse (Nobel Laureate 1946), *Narziss and Goldmund*
Rudyard Kipling (Nobel Laureate 1907), *Kim*
Naguib Mahfouz (Nobel Laureate 1988), *The Cairo Trilogy*
Gabriel García Márquez (Nobel Laureate 1982), *One Hundred Years of Solitude*
Toni Morrison (Nobel Laureate 1993), *Beloved*
Herta Müller (Nobel Laureate 2009), *The Land of Green Plums*
V.S. Naipaul (Nobel Laureate 2001), *A House for Mr. Biswas*
Boris Pasternak (Nobel Laureate 1958), *Doctor Zhivago*
Isaac Bashevis Singer (Nobel Laureate 1978), *The Family Moskat*
Sigrid Undset (Nobel Laureate 1928), *Kristin Lavransdatter*
Patrick White (Nobel Laureate 1973), *Voss*

JIM CRACE (b. 1946)

SIGNALS OF DISTRESS (1994)

Winifred Holtby Memorial Prize 1994

Jim Crace is one of the most original English novelists of his generation. Whether imagining life in a Stone Age village (*The Gift of Stones*) or re-casting the story of Christ's sojourn in the wilderness into a new narrative (*Quarantine*), he possesses an ability to surprise his readers and he uses his distinctive and carefully-crafted prose style to fashion stories unlike those of any of his contemporaries. Perhaps his most startling and unusual book is *Being Dead* in which a middle-aged couple, re-visiting the beach where they first made love thirty years before, become victims of a random killer. Crace charts the slow decomposition of their undiscovered bodies with a dispassionate meticulousness that creates an odd but moving meditation on love and mortality. By contrast, *Signals of Distress* is a much more conventional work. It is an historical novel, set in an English coastal town in the 1830s. Its central character is Aymer Smith, a shy, repressed, rather pompous bachelor, who arrives in Wherrytown to bring difficult news that his family soap-making firm, thanks to technological change, will no longer be trading with the kelp-gatherers in the town. Coincident with Aymer's arrival in Wherrytown, an American sailing ship, with its crew and passengers, has also made an unscheduled stop there. Aymer is attracted to one of the passengers, a newly married woman awaiting passage to Canada, and dreams of romance while clashing with the Wherrytowners, over his clumsy attempts to ease the blow of the news he brings, and with the ship's captain, over a black slave he helps to escape. The book shares with Crace's more offbeat works an interest in the inevitable collision of different worlds. Aymer's well-meaning but blundering attempts to communicate with the Wherrytowners and with the Americans are doomed to failure. The signals all sides send out are lost in the sending.

☙ Read on

Being Dead; *Quarantine*
Melvyn Bragg, *The Maid of Buttermere*; Tracy Chevalier, *Falling Angels*; Robert Edric, *Gathering the Water*

LOUIS DE BERNIÈRES (b. 1954) UK

CAPTAIN CORELLI'S MANDOLIN (1994)

Commonwealth Writers' Prize 1995

After working as a teacher, Louis de Bernières began his career as a novelist with three books (*The War of Don Emmanuel's Nether Parts*, *Señor Vivo and the Coca Lord* and *The Troublesome Offspring of Cardinal Guzman*) that were heavily influenced by magic realism and set in South America. On the strength of these South American novels, he was chosen as one of the *Granta* twenty Young British Novelists in 1993 (others on the list included ❯❯ Lawrence Norfolk and ❯❯ Tibor Fischer) and the following year he published a bestseller which marked a change of direction in both style and subject matter. This was *Captain*

Corelli's Mandolin. In the Second World War the Greek island of Cephallonia is occupied by an Italian force led by the amiable and civilised Captain Antonio Corelli. More interested in music and his mandolin than he is in potential military glory, Corelli is a gentlemanly invader. His response to a barked 'Heil Hitler' is the far more agreeable 'Heil Puccini.' Drawn into the world of the Cephallonians, he embarks on an intense love affair with a local doctor's daughter, Pelagia. Yet, as the war goes on, its horrors draw ever closer. Pelagia's first lover, the fisherman Mandras, who had gone off to fight, returns and he has been transformed into a bitter and ruthless man. The Germans turn upon their erstwhile allies, the Italians. Different groups of resistance fighters and guerrillas battle for the soul of Greece and the right to determine its future after the war. The love between Corelli and Pelagia is threatened by all those forces which care nothing for the individual and his or her happiness. The political and the personal become ever more difficult to disentangle and, as ordinary people are caught up in the larger forces of history, tragedy becomes inevitable.

Film version: *Captain Corelli's Mandolin* (starring Nicolas Cage as Corelli and Penelope Cruz as Pelagia)

Read on

The War of Don Emmanuel's Nether Parts (the first of three loosely-connected novels published before *Captain Corelli's Mandolin*); *Birds Without Wings*; *A Partisan's Daughter*

Sebastian Faulks, *Charlotte Gray*; ≫ Barry Unsworth, *Pascali's Island*

SEAMUS DEANE (b. 1940) UK

READING IN THE DARK (1996)

Guardian Fiction Prize 1996

Primarily a poet and critic, Seamus Deane has published a number of volumes of his verse over the last forty years, and non-fiction works that have ranged from a short history of Irish literature to a book about the impact of the French Revolution in England. He has also been an editor on the influential *Field Day Review* of Irish literature. *Reading in the Dark* is his only novel and a haunting and haunted work it is. Its narrator, looking back on his boyhood and trying to make sense of growing up in Derry in the 1940s and 1950s, realises that he was haunted by the local stories and folk tales he hears – of the field of the disappeared over which no bird will fly, of the house where children are seized by the ghosts of their parents, of the ancient fort where warriors lie sleeping, awaiting the call to awake and drive the English from Ireland – and by his developing awareness that his own family is in thrall to events in the past, to political enmities and betrayals and to secrets shared and not shared. The boy's Uncle Eddie was a member of the IRA but disappeared during a fire at a distillery in the Irish Civil War. In family legend, Eddie either died amidst the flames or ended up far from Ireland, glimpsed years later in Chicago. Yet the mystery of Eddie's disappearance and the question of whether or not he might have been an informer hang still over his relatives. 'So broken was my father's family,' according to the narrator, 'that it felt to me like a catastrophe you could live with only if you kept it quiet.' As the boy slowly pieces together the fragments of his family's history, he begins to understand just what the unspoken pact of silence about the past means.

🔖 Read on

Roddy Doyle, *Paddy Clarke Ha Ha Ha*; Anne Enright, *The Gathering*

KIRAN DESAI (b. 1971) INDIA

THE INHERITANCE OF LOSS (2006)

Man Booker Prize 2006

In 2006, Kiran Desai, daughter of the well-known novelist Anita Desai, became the youngest woman to win the Man Booker Prize. Her first novel, *Hullabaloo in the Guava Orchard*, had appeared eight years earlier and was a comedy about an Indian post office worker who gains an unmerited reputation as a religious guru. It attracted much praise from readers and reviewers, including ❯❯ Salman Rushdie who called it 'welcome proof that India's encounter with the English language continues to give birth to new children, endowed with lavish gifts.' *The Inheritance of Loss* was her second book. Jemubhai Potatlal is an elderly judge, retired and living in a crumbling Raj-era mansion in Kalimpong, a town in the foothills of the Himalayas, with his orphaned granddaughter Sai. Sai is sixteen years old and more than half in love with one of her tutors, Gyan, a handsome young Nepalese from a poor background. In addition to grandfather and granddaughter, the third important member of the household is the cook whose son, Biju, is living in the USA. In another strand to Desai's narrative, readers see Biju struggling to earn a living in New York and trying to stay one jump ahead of the immigration services which might expel him. In Kalimpong, as well, there is trouble for Desai's characters. The period is the 1980s and the ethnic Nepalese in the region, poor and powerless, are in rebellion against the Indian government. Not only is the grumpy and intolerant old judge a likely target for the rebels but Gyan is also in sympathy with their aims and has thrown in his lot with them. As Desai weaves together the two threads of her narrative, all of the central characters in the novel are forced to face up to unpleasant truths in their lives.

☙ Read on

Hullabaloo in the Guava Orchard
Anita Desai, *The Village by the Sea*

JUNOT DIAZ (b. 1968) DOMINICAN REPUBLIC/USA

THE BRIEF WONDROUS LIFE OF OSCAR WAO
(2007)

Pulitzer Prize for Fiction 2008

Born in the Dominican Republic, Junot Diaz moved to the US as a child to join his father and went on to gather degrees from Rutgers and Cornell universities. He began publishing his short fiction in the mid-1990s and these were published in *Drown*, a much-acclaimed collection in 1996. Admirers of his work had to wait more than a decade for his first novel to appear but, when it did, it won the Pulitzer, still the most prestigious of all prizes for US fiction. *The Brief Wondrous Life of Oscar Wao* begins with two epigraphs, one from Marvel Comics' Fantastic Four and one from the West Indian poet Derek Walcott, an indication of Diaz's determination to mingle popular culture with more highbrow fare in his expansive tale of his eponymous hero's difficult journey into adulthood. Oscar is an overweight and geekish Dominican-American living in Paterson, New Jersey with aspirations as a fantasy writer and a love life that never seems to take off. Spiralling outwards and backwards from Oscar's travails, Diaz's narrator, later revealed to be Oscar's room-mate at university, another Dominican named Yunior, relates the histories of other members of the family. We learn of the experiences of Oscar's mother, Beli, and her father, Abelard, in the madhouse that was the Dominican Republic under the long dictatorship of the half-demented Rafael Trujillo and the events which led Beli to join the Dominican diaspora and emigrate to New York. Eventually, Oscar's life looks as if it might be but the culmination of generations of bad luck to have afflicted the Caribbean in general and his own family in particular. Told in a rich and energetic prose that jumps from profanity to erudition, from formal English to Spanish slang, in the space of a few short sentences, *The Brief Wondrous Life of Oscar Wao* is, in the words of one American critic, 'an immigrant-family saga for people who don't read immigrant family-sagas.'

🕮 Read on

Drown

Nathan Englander, *The Ministry of Special Cases*; Oscar Hijuelos, *The Mambo Kings Play Songs of Love*

E.L. DOCTOROW (b. 1931) USA

THE MARCH (2005)

PEN/Faulkner Award for Fiction 2005

E.L. Doctorow, born in New York, the son of a family of Russian-Jewish descent, is one of the most widely admired novelists in the USA of his generation. His best-known novel, first published in the 1970s, is *Ragtime*, in which fictional characters and real individuals from early twentieth-century American history meet and interact on the page. In the decades since the appearance of *Ragtime*, Doctorow has continued to attract critical acclaim and to find his own ambivalent form of inspiration in his country's past. *Billy Bathgate* (which won the Pen/Faulkner Award in 1990) is the story of a fatherless teenager in the Bronx who becomes a surrogate son to the mobster Dutch Schulz; his most recent novel, *Homer and Langley*, takes the real lives of two eccentric New York brothers in the 1930s and 1940s and turns them into compelling fiction. *The March*, the second novel to win Doctorow the PEN/Faulkner Award, focuses on General Sherman's Union Army as it marches through Georgia and the Carolinas in the last days of the American Civil War, spreading death and destruction as it goes. Using the same techniques that he did in *Ragtime*, Doctorow builds up his novel through a series of short vignettes but its cumulative effect is very powerful. Characters both real and imagined are brought to life, from William Tecumseh Sherman himself to Pearl, the teenage daughter of a white plantation owner and one of his slaves, who disguises herself as a drummer boy amidst the chaos, and Wrede Sartorius, a field surgeon in the invading army who becomes fascinated by a soldier nursing a strange neurological injury. Gradually, from dozens of snapshots, a picture emerges of the extraordinary historical event in the shadow of which ordinary people are endeavouring to survive and create their own stories.

🎴 Read on
Billy Bathgate; *Homer and Langley*; *Ragtime*
Geraldine Brooks, *March*; Michael Shaara, *The Killer Angels*

HELEN DUNMORE (b. 1952) UK

A SPELL OF WINTER (1995)

Orange Prize for Fiction 1996

Helen Dunmore is an exceptionally versatile writer who has published poetry, volumes of short stories and children's fiction as well as nearly a dozen novels. These vary enormously in their settings. Her first adult novel, *Zennor in Darkness,* follows the fortunes of D.H. Lawrence and his German-born wife as they provoke suspicion and fear in the Cornish countryside during the First World War. *The Siege* takes place in Leningrad during the worst days of the Second World War. *Counting the Stars* is a clever reconstruction of ancient Rome and the love affair between the poet Catullus and the enigmatic noblewoman Clodia. More than one of her novels uses the genre of the psychological thriller to explore the tensions of sexual relationships and family life. *A Spell of Winter*, which won the Orange Prize in the first year it was awarded, is set in Edwardian England and borrows elements of melodrama and the most sinister of fairytales in its story of a traumatised family. The book tells of the intensifying intimacy between a brother and sister (Rob and Catherine) left to their own devices when their mother deserts them and their father descends into madness. Living in isolation in an eerily described country home, Rob and Catherine take comfort in an incestuous relationship. She becomes pregnant and endures a gruesomely described abortion. The terrible tensions of the household, brilliantly evoked by Dunmore, build and build until events outside the claustrophobic clutch of the family break in. The outbreak of the First World War and the events that follow finally free first Rob and then Catherine from the ties that have bound them. A compelling exploration of innocence and corruption, Dunmore's tale of a household riddled with secrets and undercurrents of violence is a memorable rewriting of the classic Gothic novel for a modern readership.

🕮 Read on
With Your Crooked Heart; *House of Orphans*
Jane Gardam, *God on the Rocks*; Lesley Glaister, *Honour Thy Father*

MARGUERITE DURAS (1914–96) FRANCE

THE LOVER (1984)

Prix Goncourt 1984

Born near Saigon at a time when what is now Vietnam was under French colonial rule, Marguerite Donnadieu returned to France in her teens and was active in the French Resistance during the war. Taking the pen name of Duras from that of a village where her father had owned property, she went on to become a prolific writer of fiction, much of it revisiting and reshaping her own past. Well-known works include *Moderato Cantabile*, the story of a wealthy woman who becomes obsessed by a *crime passionel* and returns again and again to the cafe where it took place, and the screenplay for the legendary French new wave film of 1959, *Hiroshima Mon Amour*. *The Lover*, published when Duras was in her seventies, is an autobiographical novel set in French colonial Indochina and focusing on the affair between a teenage girl from a French family and an older, wealthier man. The period is the 1920s and the fifteen-year-old central character is on a ferry travelling back to her boarding school in Saigon when she falls into conversation with the son of a Chinese businessman. The man is twelve years older than she is but their meeting is the starting point of an intense relationship that ends only when, under pressure from his disapproving father, he breaks it off. The girl, rebellious and disaffected with her emotionally disturbed mother and troublesome brothers, acquiesces in the affair but seems strangely detached. Only in her later years can she acknowledge the significance it had for her. The plot of the book is slight but the lyrical beauty and eloquence of the language in which

Duras relates her story of love and loss and memory are undeniable. *The Lover* is, as one critic described it, 'an exquisite jewel of a novel, as multifaceted as a diamond, as seamless and polished as a pearl'.

🎬 **Film version:** *L'Amant* (1992, directed by Jean-Jacques Annaud)

📖 **Read on**
Moderato Cantabile
Simone de Beauvoir, *She Came to Stay*; ›› Michael Ondaatje, *The English Patient*

UMBERTO ECO (b. 1932) ITALY
THE NAME OF THE ROSE (1980)
Premio Strega 1981

Before publishing his first novel in Italian in his late forties, Umberto Eco was already a well-known figure in the Italian intellectual and cultural world. Beginning as a medievalist with a particular interest in Thomas Aquinas, Eco moved into the emerging field of semiotics and became the first professor of the subject at one of Europe's oldest universities, Bologna. Since its first publication, *The Name of the Rose* has sold millions of copies worldwide and it launched Eco on a parallel career as a novelist. The story is set in the fourteenth century and is told by Adso of Melk, an aged monk looking back on his youthful experiences when he took shelter at a remote Italian monastery with his companion, Brother William of Baskerville, a Franciscan friar committed to the use of logic and reason to understand the world. Whilst they are staying at the monastery several monks meet with bizarre deaths. (One is found head-down in a vessel of pig's blood.) Brother William pits his wits against the killer and realises that the key to the whole mystery lies with the labyrinthine library at the heart of the abbey and with its custodian, the blind scholar Jorge of Burgos. Eventually, through the application of deductive abilities which anticipate those of Sherlock Holmes, he comes close to the truth. *The Name of the Rose* works on its simplest level as a page-turning crime novel. The reader hastens towards its end, eager to learn the identity of the murderer and his reasons for committing his crimes. However, the story of William of Baskerville and his investigations also becomes a study of the nature of truth and of the various ways in which ordinary, fallible human beings can struggle to understand it. The villain of the piece comes to represent all those in history who wish to impose truth from above and prevent people from freely exercising their imaginations and their intellects. Brother William, by contrast, emerges as the hero of a tale that celebrates tolerance and open-mindedness and the willingness to laugh at ourselves.

🎬 **Film version:** *The Name of the Rose* (directed by Jean-Jacques Annaud and starring Sean Connery as William of Baskerville)

📚 **Read on**
Foucault's Pendulum; *Baudolino*
Luther Blissett, *Q*: Italo Calvino, *Our Ancestors*; Iain Pears, *An Instance of the Fingerpost*

READONATHEME: CRIME FICTION AWARD WINNERS

There are many awards for crime fiction worldwide but the most prestigious are probably the Gold Dagger and the International Dagger, given by the British Crime Writers' Association, and the Edgar Awards, named after Edgar Allan Poe, which are awarded by the Mystery Writers of America

Lawrence Block, *A Dance at the Slaughterhouse* (Edgar Award for Best Novel 1992)

James Lee Burke, *Black Cherry Blues* (Edgar Award for Best Novel 1990)

Patricia Cornwell, *Postmortem* (Edgar Award for Best First Novel 1991)

Joe R. Lansdale, *The Bottoms* (Edgar Award for Best Novel 2001)

Elmore Leonard, *LaBrava* (Edgar Award for Best Novel 1984)

Henning Mankell, *Sidetracked* (CWA Gold Dagger Award 2001)

Eliot Pattison, *The Skull Mantra* (Edgar Award for Best First Novel 2000)

Ian Rankin, *Black and Blue* (CWA Gold Dagger Award 1997)

Martin Cruz Smith, *Gorky Park* (CWA Gold Dagger Award 1981)

Fred Vargas, *Wash This Blood Clean From My Hand* (CWA International Dagger 2007)

Barbara Vine, *King Solomon's Carpet* (CWA Gold Dagger Award 1991)

Minette Walters, *The Scold's Bride* (CWA Gold Dagger Award 1994)

JOSHUA FERRIS (b. 1974) USA

THEN WE CAME TO THE END (2007)

Hemingway Foundation/PEN Award for First Novel 2008

Told, unusually for a novel, in the third person plural, *Then We Came to the End* is a satirical exposé of the American workplace. 'We were fractious and overpaid,' Ferris begins as he introduces readers to the fictional Chicago ad agency where his multi-stranded story unfolds. 'Our mornings lacked promise. At least those of us who smoked had something to look forward to at ten-fifteen.' The workers at the agency seem at first indistinguishable, one from another. All are obsessed with their fluctuating status within the hierarchy. All worry endlessly about what their workaholic boss Lynn Mason might think of them. All fret ceaselessly about the wave of redundancies that might break over any one of them at any minute. Gradually, characters begin to emerge from the collective 'we' of the narrative voice. There is Chris Yop, a desperate middle-aged copywriter so convinced that he will never get another job that he continues to work on advertising campaigns after he has been fired in the hope that this will persuade the agency to rehire him. There is Joe Pope, Lynn Mason's right-hand man, who seems so aloof that everyone resents him. There is Benny Shassburger who is bequeathed a Native American totem pole in the will of an ex-colleague and doesn't know what to do with it. As they struggle to deal with real or imagined crises in the workplace – the possibility that Lynn Mason may have breast cancer and not be telling anyone, the chance that Tom Mota, a disgruntled ex-employee, might return to the building in murderous mood – readers are drawn into their world. Often bitingly funny and always perceptive, *Then We Came to The End* reminds us that we spend so much of our time at work that we should really learn to understand more about what happens there.

🐟 Read on
The Unnamed
Don DeLillo, *Americana*; Ted Heller, *Slab Rat*

TIBOR FISCHER (b. 1959) UK
UNDER THE FROG (1992)
Betty Trask Award 1992

Tibor Fischer, born in Britain to Hungarian parents, has published five novels in his career. These have ranged from *The Thought Gang*, a dazzling display of linguistic and intellectual fireworks which tells the unlikely story of an out-of-work philosopher joining forces with a one-armed robber in a crime spree through France, to *Good to Be God*, a tale of an unsuccessful con artist arriving in Miami and attempting to persuade its more gullible citizens that, despite all appearances, He is the Supreme Being. Fischer was selected as one of *Granta* magazine's Twenty Best of Young British Novelists in 1993 and his recent fiction has many admirers but it was his debut novel that was shortlisted for the

Booker Prize. It also went on to win a Betty Trask award for a first work of fiction. *Under the Frog* takes its title from a Hungarian saying. To be 'under the frog's arse down a coal mine' means, as one might guess, to be at a low point in one's life. It is a picaresque story of the adventures of two Hungarians, Pataki and Gyuri, as they tour their country with a national basketball team in the years between the end of the Second World War and the Hungarian uprising in 1956. Trapped in the everyday lunacies of totalitarianism, the two young men and their team-mates are interested primarily in sex, drink, food and maintaining their place in the squad. Outside the cocoon of the team and the special train on which it travels swirls the madness of the communist regime. As the unrest in the country develops into a full-scale rebellion against the Soviet-backed government, the two disaffected young men find themselves forced to choose sides. Blackly comic and linguistically inventive, *Under the Frog* is a book that invites us to mock the pretensions and follies of totalitarian regimes unmercifully without allowing us to forget the brutal realities of power on which they are based.

🍃 Read on

The Thought Gang; *Voyage to the End of the Room*
Andrey Kurkov, *Death and the Penguin*

GILES FODEN (b. 1967) UK

THE LAST KING OF SCOTLAND (1998)

Betty Trask Award 1999

Giles Foden has published four novels, all but one of them set in Africa, the continent in which he spent much of his childhood. *Ladysmith* is an ambitious historical novel focusing on the siege of the town of that name which was one of the central events of the Boer War; in *Zanzibar*, he moves forward in time to the end of the twentieth century and constructs a complex moral thriller around the 1998 bombing of the US embassy in Tanzania. *The Last King of Scotland* was his debut novel. It tells the story of Nicholas Garrigan, a young Scottish doctor who moves to Uganda in the 1970s. Working in a bush surgery, he is asked to attend to a man who has sprained his wrist in an accident involving a red Maserati car and a large cow. The man is Idi Amin, the country's ruler. A few months later, Garrigan receives a letter from the Minister of Health, summoning him to Kampala to take up the post of Amin's personal physician. From this position, the doctor becomes a privileged witness to the worst excesses of the regime. Garrigan is appalled by Amin and his grotesque brutalities but he is simultaneously fascinated by him. As his ambivalence grows he is drawn ever deeper into complicity with the savagery he sees around him and a compelling portrait emerges of the bizarre relationship that develops between the charismatic but half-insane Amin and the young doctor. Foden's most recent novel, *Turbulence*, tells the story of scientists struggling to predict the weather as Allied armies prepare for the D-Day landings and suggests that he might have turned away from Africa as a backdrop. However, as *The*

Last King of Scotland amply demonstrates, he has been able to use the often troubled history of the continent to great effect in his fiction.

◀ Film version: *The Last King of Scotland* (2006, starring James McAvoy as Nicholas Garrigan and Forest Whitaker as Idi Amin)

▷ Read on
Ladysmith; *Zanzibar*; *Turbulence*
V.S. Naipaul, *A Bend in the River*

MICHAEL FRAYN (b. 1933) UK

SPIES (2002)

Bollinger Everyman Wodehouse Prize 2002

Michael Frayn began his career as a writer of urbanely satirical columns in various newspapers and his early novels, published in the 1960s and 1970s, were in the same vein as his journalism – deft and amusing exposés of the foibles and follies of the time. For much of the 1980s and 1990s his creative energies were directed largely towards the theatre and plays such as *Noises Off* and *Copenhagen* made him one of the most admired and successful English playwrights of his generation. He returned to fiction in 1999 with *Headlong*, the often farcical story of an art historian who believes he has made the discovery of the century and sets out to try and exploit it. *Spies* followed three years later. Its central character is Stephen Wheatley who, as an old man, comes back to the suburban streets of his childhood during the Second World War. As he walks through places he hasn't visited in decades, he recalls a story in which the fantasy games he played during those years came into abrupt and painful contact with reality. The narrative returns to the past. The child Stephen and his closest friend pretend to believe that the friend's mother is a German spy. They begin to shadow her about the streets, following her on her everyday shopping trips, trailing her on her ordinary excursions from the house, even reading her diary. As Frayn's delicately and subtly written novel gradually unfolds, Stephen slowly begins to realise that his friend's mother may not be spying for the enemy but she does indeed have other secrets to hide. They are not the ones the two boys naïvely imagined her to possess but their revelation will have serious and long-lasting consequences. Often very funny, which explains the award of the Bollinger Everyman Wodehouse Prize, *Spies* is also a poignant story of a boy struggling to understand the deviousness and deceptions of the adult world.

🕮 Read on

Headlong

Mick Jackson, *Five Boys*

CHARLES FRAZIER (b. 1950) USA

COLD MOUNTAIN (1997)

National Book Award 1997

At the heart of Charles Frazier's remarkable debut novel is W.P. Inman, a Confederate soldier in the American Civil War who is weary of the fighting. As the novel opens, he is recovering from a near-fatal wound and he has spent the long weeks in his hospital bed 'picturing the old green places he recollected from home'. Eventually he decides to desert. He sets off through the war-torn landscape of North Carolina on a long, long walk home to Cold Mountain where, he hopes and believes, his beloved Ada will still be waiting for him. What he does not know is that Ada has been struggling to maintain the farmstead she has inherited after the death of her father. Throughout her upbringing, she has been sheltered from life's harsher realities and the battle to wrest a living from the land is one she is losing before the arrival of Ruby, a tough and resourceful young woman, who throws in her lot with Ada. Together, they work to bring the farm back to life. Meanwhile Inman, a character based on one of Frazier's own ancestors who had fought in the war, plods determinedly in their direction, battling against the dangers of a nation up in arms and fighting against itself.

It is notoriously difficult to write a second novel to match a first novel that has been a huge success and Frazier has discovered this for himself. *Thirteen Moons*, the story of a white frontiersman in the American West and his involvement with the fate of the Cherokee Indians, took many years to write but failed to find either the commercial success or the critical acclaim that his earlier book had enjoyed. However, *Cold Mountain*, an odyssey that embodies the persistence of love and the endurance of hope, remains one of the most moving American novels of recent decades.

Film version: *Cold Mountain* (2003, starring Jude Law as Inman and Nicole Kidman as Ada)

Read on
Thirteen Moons
David Fuller, *Sweetsmoke*

PAOLO GIORDANO (b. 1982) ITALY
THE SOLITUDE OF PRIME NUMBERS (2008)
Premio Strega 2008

Paolo Giordano is an Italian physicist who turned to writing fiction as a distraction from his scientific endeavours. His first novel, *The Solitude of Prime Numbers*, took Italy by storm, and he became the youngest ever winner of the Premio Strega, the country's most prestigious literary award, previously given to such major luminaries as Primo Levi and Umberto Eco. The book is a minimalist and melancholy portrait of two damaged people, traumatised by events in childhood, and the ways their lives unfold over a period of years. Mattia abandoned his mentally-retarded twin sister in a park and she disappeared. Haunted by guilt, he withdraws into the world of numbers and his studies. 'He wanted to tell her that the pages of the schoolbooks were all the same temperature,' Giordano writes of Mattia's obsession with mathematics and his wish to communicate this to Alice, the girl who attempts to coax him into a greater engagement with everyday reality, 'that they left time to choose, that they never hurt you and you couldn't hurt them either.' Alice is herself an outsider. Scarred physically and psychologically by a skiing accident, she becomes anorexic as she grows older. Mattia turns to self-harm as a way of punishing himself for his desertion of his sister. In a series of short vignettes, Giordano charts the lives of these two troubled people as they travel uncomfortably through adolescence and early adulthood. As Mattia says, they are like prime numbers which can only be divided by themselves and one. Or, more precisely, they are like twin primes, numbers such as 11 and 13 or 17 and 19, which differ by the smallest amount but are still forever separated. This metaphor for two lives which travel on parallel but still irreconcilable paths is at the heart of a poignant and moving debut novel.

🕮 Read on

Niccolo Ammaniti, *I'm Not Scared*

WILLIAM GOLDING (1911–93)

RITES OF PASSAGE (1980)

Booker Prize 1980

Rites of Passage is the first volume of a trilogy, published in one volume under the title of *To the Ends of the Earth*, which follows the slow progress of a ship sailing to Australia in the early years of the nineteenth century. Its narrator (and the narrator of the later volumes) is a young aristocrat named Edmund Talbot who is writing a journal of his experiences on board ship. Talbot is, in many ways, an unlikely and unlikeable hero. He is a snob, both socially and intellectually, overweeningly proud of his classical education and his connections to aristocracy. On his way to New South Wales to take up a post in the government there, he is determined that his place in the social hierarchy should be acknowledged and respected. As the ship sails ever southwards, the elements of tragedy are beginning to fall into place. Also on board is a priggish and insecure parson, from a lowly background, named Colley. At first, Colley's inability to mix with his fellow passengers and with the crew seems nothing more than a minor irritant on the voyage but, when the ship 'crosses the line', he faces a humiliation that ultimately destroys him. Golding, winner of the Nobel Prize for Literature in 1983, is well known as the author of *Lord of the Flies*, a chilling parable of man's capacity for cruelty which has been on reading lists for schools and universities for more than half a century. *Rites of Passage* won the Booker Prize in 1980, just pipping at the post Anthony Burgess's huge and hugely ambitious *Earthly Powers*, a book that many, including its author, believed to be a more deserving victor that year. Certainly Golding's novel is on a smaller scale than Burgess's epic take on twentieth-century history but it brilliantly re-works the themes of English naval fiction to explore ideas of shame, social class and snobbery.

🐚 Read on

Close Quarters; *Fire Down Below* (the other two volumes of the 'To the Ends of the Earth' trilogy); *The Spire*
Richard Hughes, *A High Wind in Jamaica*; ➤➤ Matthew Kneale, *English Passengers*

ALASDAIR GRAY (b. 1934) UK

LANARK (1981)

Saltire Society Scottish Book of the Year 1981

The universally acknowledged founding father of the renaissance in Scottish fiction over the last three decades is Alasdair Gray and his novel *Lanark* is recognised as a landmark work. The book was a long time in the making. One of its chapters began life as a short story that was runner up in a competition organised by *The Observer* in 1958. When, more than two decades later, the book was finally published, it was a baggy monster that showed the marks of the time and creative energy Gray had lavished upon it. Great novels defy précis and, by that criterion if no other, *Lanark* is a great novel. Like few other novels of the last half century it embraces both realism and fantasy. Its pages move between the two worlds of 1950s Glasgow, where its central character Duncan Thaw searches for love and meaning in his life, and of the city of Unthank, in which the dead Thaw is reincarnated as a young man who has chosen the name Lanark. The book opens in Unthank, a strange and bleak city where the sun never properly shines and where the aimless, disoriented people suffer from odd diseases. Lanark himself suffers from 'dragonhide', which covers his flesh in scaly armour. Spirited away to a sinister 'Institute' which cures his disease but holds gruesome secrets, Lanark is eventually able to consult an oracle which tells him of the life he led before Unthank. The novel shifts direction into naturalism and the story of Duncan Thaw in Glasgow. *Lanark* slowly develops into an imaginative *tour de force* in which the real and the surreal constantly collide. In the last thirty years Alasdair Gray has published some remarkable fiction – from *Poor Things*, an imaginative Victorian pastiche which tells of the creation of a kind of female Frankenstein's monster in nineteenth-century Glasgow, to *A History Maker*, his idiosyncratic version of an SF novel – but nothing has quite matched his debut in scope and originality.

☙ Read on

The Fall of Kelvin Walker; *Poor Things*
James Joyce, *Ulysses*; Jeff Torrington, *Swing, Hammer, Swing*

KATE GRENVILLE (b. 1950) AUSTRALIA

THE SECRET RIVER (2005)

Commonwealth Writers' Prize 2006

One of the subtlest and most engaging of contemporary Australian novelists, Kate Grenville has written with great insight about her country's often troubled past. *The Secret River* reconstructs the early days of white Australia and tells the story of Will and Sal Thornhill, who are transported from London to New South Wales. In the harsh sunlight of a distant land, they are forced not only to build new lives for themselves but also to confront the alarming otherness of the Aboriginal peoples already inhabiting it. Opportunity for betterment presents itself in the shape of supposedly unclaimed land up the Hawkesbury River and away from the primitive settlements of Sydney. Will is eager to establish himself as a man of property and fulfil his desire to possess a piece of land which can be 'the blank page on which a man might write a new life'. However, when he and Sal and their expanding family turn their backs on the township and move upriver, they find the land is not quite as empty as they believed. Aboriginal people are already there. As two utterly different cultures, each incapable of understanding the other, come face to face, the stage is set for tragedy. Will is a fundamentally decent man who longs for nothing more than to live in peace with all his fellow men, whether white or black, but circumstances and his less tolerant neighbours conspire to force him into making a terrible decision. The violent consequences of the decision haunt him for the rest of his life. Deservedly shortlisted for the Booker Prize in the year it was published, and the winner of several awards in

Grenville's native New South Wales, *The Secret River* is a poignant exploration of the human losses and gains involved in the creation of white Australia.

🥢 Read on

The Idea of Perfection; *The Lieutenant*
Carol Birch, *Scapegallows*; Colleen McCullough, *Morgan's Run*

DAVID GUTERSON (b. 1956) USA

SNOW FALLING ON CEDARS (1994)

PEN/Faulkner Award for Fiction 1995

David Guterson began his career as a teacher in his native Seattle and had already published a collection of short stories and a book on the benefits of home schooling before his first novel appeared when he was in his late thirties. *Snow Falling on Cedars* is set on an island off the north-west coast of America in the 1950s. A fisherman has been murdered on his boat and a man stands in the dock of the courtroom, accused of the murder. The man is Kabuo Miyamoto, a member of the large Japanese community on the island. Watching the proceedings is Ishmael Chambers, owner of the local newspaper, a lonely man whose only love has been for a woman who refused him and later became Miyamoto's wife. As the trial moves forward, with the inherent tension that courtroom dramas in fiction and film so often possess, the story also moves back in time to Chambers's failed love affair, to the war and the racial tensions it released on the island. *Snow Falling on Cedars* was a major bestseller when it was first published as well as the winner of several literary prizes in the USA. In the years since his debut novel, Guterson has published three further full-length works of fiction. His most recent novel, *The Other*, published in 2008, follows the friendship of two men over thirty years, one of whom abandons society for a life in the wilderness. All of Guterson's fiction deservedly receives respectful and often admiring review coverage but none of his novels has struck quite the same chord with readers as his first one. In *Snow Falling on Cedars*, he gradually builds up a picture of an entire community, living precariously in a harsh landscape. And he does so while both maintaining the reader's interest in the whodunit elements of his plot and exploring a drama of clashing cultures and values. For any novelist it was a major achievement. For a first novelist it was remarkable.

🎬 **Film version:** *Snow Falling on Cedars* (1999, starring Ethan Hawke as Ishmael Chambers)

📖 **Read on**
East of the Mountains; *Our Lady of the Forest*
Brunonia Barry, *The Lace Reader*; Hillary Jordan, *Mudbound*

MARK HADDON (b. 1962) UK

THE CURIOUS INCIDENT OF THE DOG IN THE NIGHT-TIME (2003)

Whitbread Book of the Year 2003

Mark Haddon was already a successful children's author and illustrator, with more than a dozen titles to his name, when he published *The Curious Incident of the Dog in the Night-Time*. Its narrator, Christopher Boone, is an autistic teenager who knows all the countries of the world and their capitals and can recite every prime number up to 7,057 but finds human emotions difficult to understand and cannot bear to be touched. He lives with his father and believes that his mother died two years before the story begins. When he chances upon the corpse of his neighbour's dog, pinned to the front lawn with a garden fork, he decides to emulate his hero Sherlock Holmes. He sets about discovering who has killed the dog and why. Although he does not know it at first, he has embarked on a quest that will lead him to discomfiting new knowledge about his own family. His father strongly discourages Christopher from pursuing his detective work and confiscates the notebook in which the boy is recording the progress of the case. While searching for it, Christopher stumbles across letters written by his mother after her supposed death. She is, in fact, living in London with the husband of the neighbour whose dog was speared by the fork. Appalled by the revelation of his father's deceit, he decides to set off on a journey to the city, made particularly perilous for him by his fears and phobias, in order to be once again with his mother. Shortlisted for the W.H. Smith Award for Fiction and the Carnegie Medal for an outstanding book for children, winner of both the Whitbread Book of the Year and the Guardian Children's Fiction Prize, Haddon's book is a touching portrait of a boy whose difference marks him out from other people but who struggles in his own unique way to make sense of the world.

🐲 Read on

A Spot of Bother
Jonathan Safran Foer, *Extremely Loud and Incredibly Close*; Daniel Keyes, *Flowers for Algernon*; Yann Martel, *Life of Pi*

READONATHEME: CHILDREN'S/YOUNG ADULTS' FICTION

David Almond, *The Fire-eaters* (Whitbread Children's Award 2003)

Melvyn Burgess, *Junk* (Carnegie Medal in Literature 1996)

Roald Dahl, *The Witches* (Whitbread Children's Award 1983)

Siobhan Dowd, *Bog Child* (Carnegie Medal in Literature 2009)

Anne Fine, *Flour Babies* (Carnegie Medal in Literature 1992)

Neil Gaiman, *The Graveyard Book* (Newbery Medal 2009)

Jamila Gavin, *Coram Boy* (Whitbread Children's Award 2000)

Janni Howker, *The Nature of the Beast* (Whitbread Children's Award 1985)

Dick King-Smith, *The Sheep-Pig* (Guardian Children's Fiction Award 1984)

Patrick Ness, *The Knife of Never Letting Go* (Guardian Children's Fiction Award 2008)

Philip Pullman, *Northern Lights* (Carnegie Medal in Literature 1995)

Louis Sachar, *Holes* (Newbery Medal 1999)

Mildred Taylor, *Roll of Thunder, Hear My Cry* (Newbery Medal 1977)

Sylvia Waugh, *The Mennyms* (Guardian Children's Fiction Award 1994)

Jacqueline Wilson, *The Illustrated Mum* (Guardian Children's Fiction Award 2000)

SARAH HALL (b. 1974) UK

THE CARHULLAN ARMY (2007)

John Llewellyn Rhys Prize 2007

Sarah Hall has only published a handful of novels yet she has already demonstrated an ability to create memorable fiction in a range of different styles and genres. *Haweswater*, her first novel, is set in the 1930s and examines the destructive impact on a small Cumbrian community of the creation of a new reservoir. She followed *Haweswater* with *The Electric Michelangelo*, another historical novel about a tattoo artist sailing from Britain to set up his stall amidst the freak shows and funfairs of Coney Island in the early years of the twentieth century. Her third book, *The Carhullan Army*, is a dystopian tale set in a ramshackle future Britain run by a dictatorship known as the Authority. The narrator, a woman known only as Sister, escapes from one of the run-down, squalid townships where most people live and goes in search of Carhullan, a communal farm run by women in the Cumbrian hills which she remembers from her childhood. Captured on the fells, she is brought before Jackie Nixon, the charismatic founder of Carhullan and slowly inducted into the life that is led there. A new freedom beckons for Sister and she learns the rhythms of a self-contained society untrammelled by the Authority's restrictions. However, she also discovers that there are prices to be paid for the freedoms of the farm. Jackie, believing Carhullan is about to come under threat from the Authority, has plans to defend it. Attack is the best form of defence and Carhullan's increasingly messianic leader is training a band of female guerrillas to descend from the hills and fight in the streets of the townships. *The Carhullan Army* is a relatively short novel but its vision of a Britain in which its characters have fundamental choices about liberty, survival and individual responsibility forced upon them is a very powerful one.

🐟 Read on

Haweswater; *How to Paint a Dead Man*

» Margaret Atwood, *The Handmaid's Tale*; Robert Edric, *Salvage*; Marge Piercy, *Woman on the Edge of Time*

READONATHEME: SCIENCE FICTION AND FANTASY AWARD WINNERS

There are many awards for science fiction and fantasy fiction. In Britain the two most coveted prizes for SF are probably the Arthur C. Clarke Award and the British Science Fiction Association Award; in the USA the Hugo Awards, named after Hugo Gernsback, the legendary founder of the pioneering SF magazine *Amazing Stories*, and the Nebula Awards, granted by the Science Fiction and Fantasy Writers of America, are the most prestigious. The World Fantasy Awards are handed out each year at the World Fantasy Convention

Iain M. Banks, *Excession* (British Science Fiction Association Award for Best Novel 1997)

Orson Scott Card, *Ender's Game* (Hugo Award for Best Novel 1986)

Michael Chabon, *The Yiddish Policemen's Union* (Nebula Award for Best Novel 2007)

Susanna Clarke, *Jonathan Strange and Mr. Norrell* (World Fantasy Award for Best Novel 2005)

Neil Gaiman, *American Gods* (Hugo Award for Best Novel 2002)

William Gibson, *Neuromancer* (Hugo Award for Best Novel 1985)

Frank Herbert, *Dune* (Nebula Award for Best Novel 1965)

Robert Holdstock, *Mythago Wood* (World Fantasy Award for Best Novel 1985)

China Miéville, *The City and the City* (British Science Fiction Association Award for Best Novel 2010)

Michael Moorcock, *Gloriana* (World Fantasy Award for Best Novel 1979)

Larry Niven, *Ringworld* (Nebula Award for Best Novel 1970)

Christopher Priest, *The Separation* (Arthur C. Clarke Award 2003)

Kim Stanley Robinson, *Red Mars* (Nebula Award for Best Novel 1993)

Vernor Vinge, *A Fire Upon the Deep* (Hugo Award for Best Novel 1993)

Connie Willis, *Doomsday Book* (Nebula Award for Best Novel 1992)

ALAN HOLLINGHURST (b. 1954) UK

THE LINE OF BEAUTY (2004)

Man Booker Prize 2004

After graduating from Oxford and working in academia, Alan Hollinghurst joined the *Times Literary Supplement* in 1982 and was its deputy editor for several years in the early 1990s. He published poetry in his twenties and went on to gain immediate acclaim as a writer of fiction with the appearance in 1988 of his first novel, *The Swimming-Pool Library*. This story of the relationship between a rich, cultured and promiscuous aristo and an ageing gay roué in pre-AIDS Britain won the Somerset Maugham Award and was described by the American writer

Edmund White as 'surely the best book about gay life yet written by an English author'. Hollinghurst has since produced three more novels. The first of these, *The Folding Star*, a dark tale of sexual obsession and unrequited fantasies focusing on a young English teacher in Belgium, was shortlisted for the Man Booker Prize. The third of them, *The Line of Beauty*, won that same prize. Opening in 1983, *The Line of Beauty* charts the progress of its central character, Nick Guest, through a Thatcherite London obsessed by money, sex and the pursuit of power. Living in the Notting Hill home of an ambitious and charming Tory MP, father of an Oxford friend, Nick is plunged into the world of power politics which he observes with an appalled fascination. In the burgeoning London gay scene he also discovers love, sex and, as the 1980s move on, the growing shadows cast by AIDS. Like all of Hollinghurst's novels, *The Line of Beauty* is written in prose of enormous elegance, panache and erudition. It seems entirely appropriate that Nick Guest, amid all the excitements of his life, is struggling to complete a Ph.D on the work of Henry James, for Hollinghurst proves himself as idiosyncratically stylish a novelist as the author of *The Portrait of a Lady* and *The Golden Bowl*.

🎬 **Film version:** *The Line of Beauty* (2006, TV mini-series)

🦜 **Read on**
The Swimming-Pool Library; *The Folding Star* (two of Hollinghurst's earlier novels)
>> Jonathan Coe, *What a Carve Up!*; Philip Hensher, *Kitchen Venom*; Jamie O'Neill, *At Swim, Two Boys*

NICK HORNBY (b. 1957) UK

HOW TO BE GOOD (2001)

W.H. Smith Award for Fiction 2002

No one in the last twenty years has been as successful as Nick Hornby at portraying the emotional confusions and immaturities of a certain kind of white middle-class male. His first major book, *Fever Pitch*, an autobiographical account of his obsession with football in general and Arsenal FC in particular, was a bestseller. The protagonists of his first two novels (*High Fidelity* and *About a Boy*) were youngish, white, middle-class urban men who might easily have been mistaken for versions of the persona Hornby presented in *Fever Pitch*.

Yet Hornby is capable of more in his fiction than revisiting territory he has investigated before and he proved this in *How To Be Good*. The central character in the novel is Katie Carr, a forty-something GP whose marriage, to David, a bilious and cynical journalist, is under pressure. However, her problems begin to multiply when her husband undergoes a 'Road to Damascus' conversion from cynicism and bitterness to 'goodness'. Under the influence of a New Age guru, a man he would previously have dismissed as a charlatan, he wants to invite the homeless to share their meals. He gives away the contents of his wallet to a beggar, donates one of the family's computers to a battered women's shelter and badgers their children into giving up their favourite toys for charity. The self-styled 'angriest man in Holloway' is transformed into a zealous do-gooder. Katie, the caring GP who has previously had little difficulty thinking of herself as a 'good' person, is now the 'bad' person in the relationship, guiltily involved in an extramarital affair and resisting David's new-found moral mission to the socially deprived. Rooted in the everyday world of north London that has been the setting for most of his books, *How To Be Good* is not only very funny (Hornby's writing usually is) but it also succeeds in exploring larger moral questions unpretentiously and yet effectively.

⮒ Read on

High Fidelity; *A Long Way Down*
Tim Lott, *White City Blue*; David Nicholls, *Starter for Ten*

KHALED HOSSEINI (b. 1965) AFGHANISTAN/USA

A THOUSAND SPLENDID SUNS (2007)

Richard and Judy Best Read of the Year 2008

Khaled Hosseini was born in Kabul, Afghanistan, the son of a diplomat, but he has lived in the USA since he was a teenager. He trained as a doctor but his life was changed dramatically by the enormous, worldwide success of his first novel, *The Kite Runner*. In this tale of a boyhood friendship destroyed during Kabul's annual kite-fighting tournament, Hosseini brilliantly counterpoints the narrative of one man's experience of guilt, loss and redemption with the bitter history of modern Afghanistan. Writers who have triumphed with a first novel often find it difficult to produce a second work of similar quality but *A Thousand Splendid Suns*, another story set in his native land, proved as great an achievement as his debut. Mariam, the illegitimate daughter of a wealthy Afghan businessman, is forced into an arranged marriage with a brutal and insensitive man and sent away to live with him in Kabul. In another house in the Afghan capital, Laila grows up in a loving and eccentric family and her future chances of happiness and fulfilment seem promising. Yet, as the country and the city descend into the violence and misery of war, these two very different women both find themselves trapped in a degrading relationship with the same man. Imprisoned by the terrors of war and by the restrictions imposed on women in a Taliban-controlled Afghanistan, Mariam and Laila have only their own resources and the growing, sister-like love between them to give them hope. As their story moves towards its climax, it is an act of heroic self-sacrifice that brings a kind of freedom to one of the women. *A Thousand Splendid Suns*, like its predecessor, describes the realities of war and suffering with fierce conviction but provides the hope that some kind of redemption and salvation can still be glimpsed in the darkness.

🕮 Read on

The Kite Runner

Steven Galloway, *The Cellist of Sarajevo*

KAZUO ISHIGURO (b. 1954)

THE REMAINS OF THE DAY (1989)

Booker Prize 1989

Born in Japan but brought up and educated in England, Kazuo Ish
has made of his fiction a mirror to reflect obliquely some of
characteristics of his two nationalities. His first two books, *A Pale View
of Hills* and *An Artist of the Floating World* were enigmatic, poetic
studies of individual Japanese trying to come to terms with the realities
of the nation's recent past. His more recent work has included *Never Let
Me Go*, which uses ideas more readily associated with science fiction
(cloning, genetic engineering) to explore love and loss, and *Nocturnes*,
a collection of short stories on musical themes. His third novel and still
his most famous book, is *The Remains of the Day*. Told in the first
person by the humourless and pernickety English butler Stevens, it
cleverly reveals the self-deceptions and moral cowardice of its narrator.
As Stevens embarks on a physical journey (through the West Country on
a motoring holiday) he also launches himself on a journey through his
memories and his past. The year is 1956 and the butler's employer for
more than thirty years, Lord Darlington, has just died. The new owner of
Darlington Hall, an American, allows Stevens to travel to Cornwall,
ostensibly to look into the possibility of re-hiring a former housekeeper
who now lives there. The book takes the shape of Stevens's journal of
his trip. Looking back on a life which has been busily self-important (his
master was at the centre of dubious pro-appeasement negotiations in
the late 1930s) Stevens cannot acknowledge that he has denied himself
true human contact and the opportunity for emotional growth. His

ility to deal with his attraction to the housekeeper Miss Kenton is
y the most obvious example of personal failures which, somewhere
eneath the cold formality of his prose, Stevens himself sadly, and
ovingly, half-recognises. His narrative becomes a subtle examination
of the kind of emotional reticence that can blight and misshape lives.

Film version: *The Remains of the Day* (1993, starring Anthony
Hopkins as Stevens and Emma Thompson as Miss Kenton)

Read on
Never Let Me Go; *When We Were Orphans*
Chang-Rae Lee, *A Gesture Life*; ›› Ian McEwan, *Enduring Love*

HOWARD JACOBSON (b. 1942) UK

THE MIGHTY WALZER (1999)

Bollinger Everyman Wodehouse Prize 2000

Howard Jacobson's first novel, published in 1983, was a riotously comic
version of campus fiction with its own, idiosyncratic energy. In the years
since the appearance of *Coming from Behind*, Jacobson has written a
further nine novels which have ranged from an inventive take on the
well-worn theme of the Englishman out of his depth in foreign climes
(*Redback*) to brutally honest sex comedy (*No More Mr Nice Guy*) and a
darkly comic exploration of sexual obsession (*The Act of Love*). His

most touching and enjoyable work, which won the Bollinger Everyman Wodehouse Prize for comic writing, is *The Mighty Walzer*. This is set in 1950s Manchester and is narrated by Oliver Walzer who is entering adolescence, with all its potential for humiliation, armed only with a champion's skill at ping pong. The young Walzer is a natural at the game, picking it up even when playing not with a bat but with a Collins Classics edition of *Dr. Jekyll and Mr. Hyde*, but the shy, book-loving teen is more interested in sex than success on the ping pong table. Ping pong is easy; dealing with women rather less so. And Oliver has further problems at home, caught between the overwhelmingly feminine world of his mother, aunts, grandmother and sisters and the inviting masculinity represented by his father, a market trader with a gift of the gab. How is he to reconcile the seemingly irreconcilable contradictions of his life? There is an autobiographical intensity forever lurking behind the surface comedy in *The Mighty Walzer* and it gives the book a real bite that it might not otherwise possess. Simultaneously celebrating and sending up both its central character and the Jewish community in which he grows up, Jacobson's comic masterpiece draws on his own memories but transmutes them into a very funny, poignant coming-of-age story.

🐦 Read on

The Making of Henry; *Kalooki Nights*
Naomi Alderman, *Disobedience*; Mordecai Richler, *The Apprenticeship of Duddy Kravitz*

CHARLES JOHNSON (b. 1948) USA

MIDDLE PASSAGE (1990)

National Book Award 1990

'Of all the things that drive men to sea, the most common disaster, I've come to learn, is women.' With this sentence, Rutherford Calhoun, the narrator of Charles Johnson's picaresque historical novel, introduces himself to readers and begins his explanation of the circumstances that lead him aboard the *Republic*, a ship sailing out of New Orleans in the spring of 1830. Rutherford is a freed and well-educated slave from Illinois, who has landed in Louisiana with plans to make his fortune and few scruples how he does so. Instead he finds himself in debt and facing the unappealing prospect of marriage to a puritanical young teacher, 'as out of place in New Orleans as Saint Teresa would be at an orgy with de Sade', who proposes to reform him. So he jumps aboard the *Republic* and is soon en route for the Guinea coast to pick up a cargo of Africans from a legendary tribe known as the Allmuseri and transport them to the slave markets of the New World. As the ship sails back towards America, the voyage degenerates into a floating nightmare. The brutal captain drives his crew to plot mutiny but the Allmuseri have their own rebellion planned. Shipwreck, murder and a desperate struggle for survival await Rutherford before he can return to New Orleans and embrace the marriage and the life he had once been so eager to avoid. *Middle Passage* is the best-known work by Charles R. Johnson, an African-American scholar, academic, novelist and short-story writer who has also written a novel based on the life of Martin Luther King (*Dreamer*). It is a book which combines elements of the sea story, the adventure yarn and the slave narrative with wide-ranging historical research to produce what one reviewer called 'a savage parable of the black experience in America'.

🐚 Read on

Dreamer; *Oxherding Tale*

Lawrence Hill, *The Book of Negroes*; ❯❯ Caryl Phillips, *Crossing the River*

EDWARD P. JONES (b. 1951) USA

THE KNOWN WORLD (2003)

Pulitzer Prize for Fiction 2004

Edward P. Jones won the Hemingway Foundation/PEN Award for his first book, a collection of short stories entitled *Lost in the City*, but it was another twelve years before his first novel was published. When it did appear, it won the Pulitzer Prize for Fiction. *The Known World* takes a troubling truth from the footnotes to the history of slavery in the United States – that there were a small number of black slave-owners in the southern states before the American Civil War – and uses it as the starting point for a wonderfully wide-ranging reconstruction of a society turned morally upside down. The focus of the book is the small plantation of Henry Townsend, a former slave who was freed as a child and grows up under the tutelage of the man who once owned him, William Robbins, the richest man in Manchester County, Virginia.

Robbins has a fondness for Henry and he sets him up with both his first parcel of land and his first slave. As Henry grows older, he prospers and is able to buy more slaves. By the time he dies, still only in his thirties, he is in a position to leave his wife Caldonia with a valuable inheritance but the terrible injustices and ironies of blacks owning blacks lurk beneath the apparently ordered surface of his estate. With Henry dead, his plantation begins to fall apart and Moses, the first slave he ever owned, begins to harbour his own ambitions for a better future. Jones creates memorable characters – Henry, a black man prepared to take possession of other black men; Robbins, an unwavering enthusiast for slavery who nonetheless saves his greatest affection for his black lover and their mulatto children – but his greatest success lies in the way he reconstructs the whole society in which they pass their lives.

🐚 Read on
All Aunt Hagar's Children (short stories)
Joan Brady, *Theory of War*; Valerie Martin, *Property*

LLOYD JONES (b. 1955) NEW ZEALAND

MISTER PIP (2006)

Commonwealth Writers' Prize 2007

In his native New Zealand, Lloyd Jones has been much admired as a writer since the publication of his first collection of short stories, *Swimming to Australia*, in 1991; in the rest of the world he was less well known until the appearance of *Mister Pip* which, as well as winning the Commonwealth Writers' Prize, was shortlisted for the 2007 Man Booker Prize. The novel is set in a village on the tropical island of Bougainville in the Pacific during a period of civil war between the islanders. The village school has fallen victim to the fighting and the children have been unable to attend it for many weeks. When it re-opens, it does so under the aegis of the island's last remaining white man, Mr. Watts, and he has but one book from which to read to his pupils – a battered copy of Charles Dickens's *Great Expectations*. The story of what happens next is told by Matilda, a woman looking back on the thirteen-year-old self who was one of those few pupils. Mr. Watts is a believer in the transformative power of literature and, through his efforts, the children glimpse another, very different world from the one in which their lives have been turned upside down by war. The Dickens novel becomes the starting point for an experiment in education into which the adults are also drawn. Pip's story becomes the catalyst for many others. Unfortunately, the war cannot be ignored. Ragged soldiers emerge from the jungle and descend on the village. Misunderstandings arise about the identity of the Mister Pip who seems to be a presence in the community and confrontation between the soldiers and Mr. Watts eventually degenerates into tragedy. Lloyd Jones's novel is a hauntingly original tale which says much about the power and the perils of storytelling in little more than two hundred pages.

🐚 Read on

The Book of Fame (offbeat fiction based on the story of the rugby-playing All-Blacks and their first tour of Britain in 1905); *Here at the End of the World We Learn to Dance*

>> Peter Carey, *Jack Maggs*; Randolph Stow, *Visitants*

SADIE JONES (b. 1967)

THE OUTCAST (2008)

Costa First Novel Award 2008

The daughter of the screenwriter Evan Jones, who produced scripts for Joseph Losey and others in the 1960s and 1970s, Sadie Jones worked for a number of years in the film world herself before she published her first novel, *The Outcast*, in 2008. The book is set in the 1950s and focuses on Lewis Aldridge who becomes a victim of the hypocrisy and repression that characterise Waterford, the fictional commuter belt town in the Home Counties where he grows up. As a boy, Lewis is traumatised by his mother's accidental drowning but he discovers that his father, who soon remarries, has little understanding of his grief. Stiff upper lipped stoicism is demanded of him at home and the neighbours want only to ignore the whole messy business. As he grows up, Lewis becomes increasingly disaffected and estranged from his father and stepmother. His grief and rage can only be expressed through self-harming, boozing and acts of minor juvenile delinquency which eventually land him in jail. As the novel opens, he is returning to Waterford to try to reconstruct his life but worse ordeals await him. Those who have already condemned him show few signs of wishing to reconsider their opinion and he is forced ever further towards the edge. Sadie Jones followed *The Outcast* with *Small Wars*, published in 2009, which also takes place in the 1950s. However, it is set not in suburbia but in Cyprus and follows the breakdown of a marriage against the backdrop of the 'small war' between the British army and the Greek Cypriots fighting to end imperial rule on the island. Both of her novels display her ability to conjure up the recent past and to create characters whose apparent ordinariness masks the kind of emotional repression that bubbles beneath the surface and eventually demands release.

⮧ Read on

Small Wars
Peter Ho Davies, *The Welsh Girl*; Kate Morton, *The House at Riverton*

A.L. KENNEDY (b. 1965) UK

DAY (2007)

Costa Book of the Year Award 2007

A.L. Kennedy writes of outsiders and grotesques, people who find it difficult or even undesirable to connect with others, people who march to the beat of very different drums and she does so in an edgy, blackly comic language. Her first published works were short stories and she has gone on to produce a number of memorable and original novels. *So I Am Glad* is narrated by Jennifer Wilson, a radio announcer determined to keep the rest of the world at bay; *Everything You Need* is set on a small island which is a retreat for writers and focuses on the developing relationship between Nathan Staples, a self-tormenting, self-obsessed middle-aged novelist and a young, would-be writer Mary who is, although she does not know it, Nathan's daughter. Kennedy's most recent novel is *Day*, which won the Saltire Society Scottish Book of the Year as well as the Costa Book of the Year Award. The book proved something of a change in direction for her in so far as it was a historical novel, set in 1949. Its central character, Alfred Day, is in northern Germany, working as an extra in a war film about a POW camp. Forlorn and wretched, surrounded by pretend prisoners, pretend guards, pretend fences, he returns to the bitter experiences of the real war which have made him the damaged man he is. 'You could dodge certain thoughts,' he tells himself, 'corkscrew off and get yourself out of their way, but they'd still hunt you.' Kennedy's novel follows the hunt as Day's thoughts slowly circle their prey. Bit by bit, with great technical skill, Kennedy unveils the personal history which drove him to join the RAF, the strange camaraderie he found there and his tale of love first found and then lost. *Day* becomes a brilliant and wholly original portrait of a man whose war has rendered him unfit for peace.

🥬 Read on

Everything You Need; *So I Am Glad*
Ali Smith, *Hotel World*; ➤➤ Alan Warner, *The Man Who Walks*

MATTHEW KNEALE (b. 1960) UK

SWEET THAMES (1992)

John Llewellyn Rhys Prize 1992

Matthew Kneale is the son of two writers (Nigel Kneale, creator of Professor Quatermass for a 1950s BBC TV series, and the children's author Judith Kerr) and began to publish his own fiction soon after graduating from Oxford. *Sweet Thames* was his third novel to be published. Set in a superbly evoked early Victorian London, it is probably the only novel ever written to have a sewage engineer as a hero. Joshua Jeavons (very loosely based on the real Victorian engineer, Sir Joseph Bazalgette) is a visionary who looks to a future London cleansed of the filth and shit and disease of its present – to what he calls 'the glory of a London unobstructed by effluent'. Working feverishly on his plans to transform the capital, Jeavons is swept into his own personal drama by the disappearance of his young wife. The book is crammed with the detail and the nitty gritty of nineteenth-century life (the mudlarks scavenging on the shore of the river, the prostitutes parading along Haymarket) but Kneale never becomes obsessed by the fruits of his research, never loses sight of a gripping, twisting plot that makes its way towards a surprising conclusion. Eight years later Kneale followed *Sweet Thames* with another historical novel set in the nineteenth century – *English Passengers*. This story of an ill-fated voyage to Tasmania in the 1850s, led by a fundamentalist clergyman determined to discover the Garden of Eden in the southern hemisphere and thus prove the literal truth of the Bible, is now his best-known work. It was shortlisted for the Booker Prize and went on to be chosen as the Whitbread Book of the Year. It is indeed a fine novel but it should not be allowed to overshadow Kneale's earlier venture into the past which fully deserved its own accolade.

🕮 Read on

English Passengers; *Small Crimes in an Age of Abundance*
>> Peter Ackroyd, *Dan Leno and the Limehouse Golem*; Robert Edric, *Elysium*

HARI KUNZRU (b. 1969) UK

THE IMPRESSIONIST (2002)

Betty Trask Award 2002

Hari Kunzru's first novel, *The Impressionist*, is set in the years of the Raj and its central character, its young anti-hero Pran Nath, is an embodiment of the contradictions and complexities of empire. Half-English and half-Indian, the boy is exiled from the comfortable life into which he was born when the truth about his parentage is revealed but he seizes upon a series of opportunities to reinvent himself. His androgynous beauty turns him into a pawn in the Machiavellian political scheming and sexual shenanigans at the court of a minor maharajah. In Bombay, he enters upon a double life when he is adopted by a Scottish missionary and his wife. To the pious couple he is a dutiful son named Robert; in the red light districts of the city to which he escapes he becomes Pretty Bobby, errand boy and part-time pimp. As political unrest grows, and the city descends into riot and bloodshed, he undertakes what he thinks will be his final metamorphosis by adopting the persona of an English teenager, destined for public school and Oxford back in England's green and pleasant land. Pran Nath is, of course, the chameleon-like 'impressionist' of the title, the man who 'becomes these other people so completely that nothing of his own is visible'. The novel is both picaresque comedy and an intelligent, subtle examination of shifting notions of self and identity. The year after *The Impressionist* was published, Hari Kunzru was chosen as one of *Granta* magazine's twenty Best of Young British Novelists and he has since produced two further novels (*Transmission*, about an Indian programmer arriving in America's Silicon Valley; *My Revolutions*, in which a middle-aged Englishman finds his violent and politically radical past returns to haunt him) and a collection of short stories (*Noise*). His status as one of the liveliest and sharpest of contemporary novelists is assured.

⮞ Read on

Transmission; *My Revolutions*
David Davidar, *The Solitude of Emperors*; Amitav Ghosh, *The Glass Palace*; Indra Sinha, *Animal's People*

HANIF KUREISHI (b. 1954) UK

THE BUDDHA OF SUBURBIA (1990)

Whitbread First Novel Award 1990

Hanif Kureishi first reached a large audience in 1985 when his screenplay *My Beautiful Laundrette* was made into a compelling film by director Stephen Frears. Other screenplays followed (*Sammy and Rosie Get Laid*, *London Kills Me*) and he also turned his attention to prose fiction, publishing a debut novel, *The Buddha of Suburbia*, in 1990. In the last twenty years much of Kureishi's creative energy has gone into prose fiction, although he has continued to write for the screen – both cinema and TV. He has proved a particularly effective writer of short stories – collections such as *Love in a Blue Time* and *The*

Body and Other Stories provide ample proof of this – and he has published several more novels. He has also written *My Ear at his Heart*, a poignant memoir exploring his relationship with his father. Yet *The Buddha of Suburbia* has long been his best-known book, its popularity only increased by the 1993 TV adaptation. Karim is a teenager growing up in the suburbs in 1970s England, the son of an Indian father and an English mother. As well as the usual challenges adolescence imposes, he is also faced by those his family and his background provide. His father, after years of trying to be more English than the English, has chosen to become a New Age guru – the Buddha of the title – and leaves his wife for one of his glamorous admirers. Through his father's lover and her rock musician son, Karim is pitched into a new world of parties, drugs and bisexual opportunities. Moving with chameleon-like adaptability from one role to another, Karim searches for a more permanent sense of self and identity. Sexy, funny and sharply satirical in its mockery of many aspects of English society, *The Buddha of Suburbia* is a traditional English comedy of manners with very untraditional characters and settings.

📚 Read on
The Black Album; *Gabriel's Gift*
Farrukh Dhondy, *Bombay Duck*; ➤➤ Zadie Smith, *White Teeth*

JOHN LANCHESTER (b. 1962) UK

THE DEBT TO PLEASURE (1996)

Betty Trask Award 1996

The Debt to Pleasure begins with the narrator's archly ironic statement, 'This is not a conventional cookbook.' What follows is not a conventional first novel. Constructed around a sequence of menus, the book begins as an apparent memoir of its narrator, gourmet and aesthete Tarquin Winot, centred on his love and knowledge of food and cooking. Self-consciously erudite and civilised, Tarquin seems, at first, a harmless food snob with a fondness for heavy irony, arcane information and baroquely extravagant language. As the book progresses, however, Lanchester slowly and subtly allows his unreliable narrator to reveal a monstrous egotism. Hiding beneath the surface are dark secrets and facts that demand explanations other than those which Tarquin supplies to readers. His parents are dead in a mysterious accident. His brother was a famous sculptor (although Tarquin thought his work tasteless kitsch) and he too is dead. Winot seems now to be stalking a honeymoon couple as they all journey through France and his reasons for wishing them anything but well gradually emerge. By the time we reach the last pages of *The Debt to Pleasure* we know we are in the company of a man whose selfishness and self-obsession have led to terrible deeds. Lanchester has published only two further novels in the years since his blackly comic debut. *Mr Phillips* is the story, told in a deliberately flat and unflamboyant narrative voice, of a day in the life of an ordinary Londoner who has been made redundant and has yet to pluck up the courage to admit this to his wife; *Fragrant Harbour* unfolds the history of Hong Kong in the twentieth century as seen through the eyes of three very different immigrants to the island. Neither of them has received quite the acclaim of *The Debt to Pleasure* (although *Fragrant Harbour* won the James Tait Black Memorial Prize) but, in different ways, they amply confirmed the talent Lanchester displayed in his bravura debut.

🐦 Read on

Mr Phillips; *Fragrant Harbour*
Vladimir Nabokov, *Lolita*

ANDREA LEVY (b. 1956) UK

SMALL ISLAND (2004)

Orange Prize 2004

Born in London to Jamaican parents, Andrea Levy has written fiction which focuses on black experience in Britain. Her first novel, *Every Light in the House Burnin'*, was published in 1994 and told the story of Angela Jacob, an ordinary young woman brought up on a London council estate, forced to cope with the fear and anxiety of her father's painful struggle against cancer. As her life narrows to hospital visits and conversations with doctors, she finds her mind returning to her childhood in the 1960s. This was followed by two further novels – *Never Far From Nowhere*, about two sisters whose lives take different paths, and *Fruit of the Lemon*, about a young Londoner learning surprising truths about her family history on a trip to Jamaica. These books were all well-reviewed but Levy's profile as a writer was raised significantly when her fourth novel, *Small Island*, won the 2004 Orange Prize for fiction. A BBC TV adaptation of the book in 2009 created an even bigger audience for Levy's story. *Small Island* is set in 1948 at the time when the first wave of immigrants from the Caribbean is arriving in London. Among them is Gilbert Joseph from Jamaica. Hortense, his new wife, soon follows but, armed with a teaching diploma and expecting an England similar to the fantasy land she has constructed in her mind, she is doomed to disappointment. Gilbert, with wartime experience of living in London, has more realistic expectations but is gradually worn down by the prejudice and misunderstandings he faces. In counterpoint to their lives, Levy shows us the world of Queenie Bligh, their formidable landlady, and her husband, Bernard, only recently returned to London after disappearing during the war. Her novel is a brilliant reconstruction of a vanished London and a memorable portrait of immigrants struggling to adapt to their new country.

Film version: *Small Island* (2009, TV mini-series)

Read on

The Long Song; *Never Far From Nowhere*

>> Caryl Phillips, *The Final Passage*; Sam Selvon, *The Lonely Londoners*

MARINA LEWYCKA (b. 1946) UK

A SHORT HISTORY OF TRACTORS IN UKRAINIAN
(2005)

Bollinger Everyman Wodehouse Prize 2005

'Two years after my mother died, my father fell in love with a glamorous blonde Ukrainian divorcée. He was eighty-four and she was thirty-six.' With these eye-catching opening lines, Marina Lewycka sets in motion her offbeat and unusual comedy, much of which takes place in Peterborough, not a city that often appears in English literary fiction. The narrator of the story and anxious observer of her father's late-flowering love affair is Nadezhda, a college lecturer from a Ukrainian family that settled in the UK immediately after the war. To her father, the blonde bombshell Valentina seems initially the ideal partner for his declining years; to Nadezhda she is clearly a gold-digger whose only interest in the old man is the opportunity he offers her to gain residence in Britain. She joins forces with her estranged elder sister Vera to thwart Valentina but the campaign to save their father from her clutches proves to be a long and arduous one. And, in the course of it, family secrets begin to bubble to the surface. 'I had thought this story was going to be a knockabout farce,' Nadezhda notes at one point, 'but now I see it is developing into a knockabout tragedy.' The shadow of events from the past still hangs over her father and her sister. Taking its unusual title from a book that Nadezhda's father, a retired engineer, is writing, *A Short History Of Tractors in Ukrainian* was Martina Lewycka's first novel, published when she was approaching sixty. She has since published two further works of fiction. *Two Caravans* investigates the lives of exploited migrant workers in the English countryside; *We Are All Made of Glue* is the story of an unlikely friendship between an elderly Jewish eccentric and a younger woman and its consequences. With the same blend of black comedy and poignantly exact observation that marked her debut, they have confirmed Lewycka's originality and talent as a novelist.

🐚 Read on

Two Caravans; *We Are All Made of Glue*

Paul Torday, *Salmon Fishing in the Yemen*; Mary Ann Shaffer, *The Guernsey Literary and Potato Peel Pie Society*

JONATHAN LITTELL (b. 1967) USA/FRANCE

THE KINDLY ONES (2006)

Prix Goncourt 2006

Jonathan Littell, the son of thriller writer Robert Littell, was brought up bilingually in France and the USA and his vast, thousand-page tale of an SS officer's experiences in the war, *The Kindly Ones*, was published originally in French. It won glowing reviews and several literary prizes in France, including the Prix Goncourt, the most prestigious of all. When it was translated into English and published in the UK, the critics were divided. Some echoed their French counterparts and used words like 'genius' and 'masterpiece' when discussing it. Others were dismissive –

one reviewer described the book as 'so bloatedly inept that its reverential reception across the Channel seems barely comprehensible'. The book is written as if it was an autobiographical work by the central character, Maximilien Aue, a former SS officer. It opens many years after the Second World War in northern France where Aue is living as he begins his act of remembrance. In the opening pages his memoir uses a commonplace justification for his part in Nazi atrocities – that he behaved only as anyone else would have behaved in the same circumstances. 'I live, I do what is possible,' he says, 'it is the same for everyone, I am a man like the others, I am a man like you. Come along, I tell you, I am like you.' His limited *mea culpa* is one that becomes increasingly difficult to accept as Littell unfolds his character's involvement in the most terrible of deeds, from the massacres of Jews by *Einsatzgruppen* death squads in Ukraine to the organisation of slave labour forces later in the war. Intermingled with the description of his public career in the SS are his records of his personal life – his homosexuality, his nervous breakdown, his incestuous feelings for his twin sister, the mysterious killings of his mother and his stepfather. Disturbing, violent and scatological, *The Kindly Ones* is an epic account of men at their worst.

ᘐ Read on

Roberto Bolano, *2666*; Bernhard Schlink, *The Reader*

ANDREI MAKINE (b. 1957) RUSSIA/FRANCE

LE TESTAMENT FRANCAIS (1995)

Prix Goncourt 1995

Born in the Soviet Union, Makine travelled to France as part of a teacher exchange programme in the 1980s and never returned, living rough at one time in the Père Lachaise cemetery in Paris and eventually seeking political asylum in his new country. His first novels in French were published as if they were translations from Russian (publishers refused to believe that someone could write so brilliantly in a language that was not his own) and it was only with his third book that the pretence was abandoned and Makine was in a position to be acknowledged as a master of his adopted tongue. *Le Testament Français*, sometimes translated into English as *Dreams of My Russian Summers*, is a semi-autobiographical work in which the narrator is caught between two cultures, the Soviet Union in which he is growing up, and the world of a long-vanished France, conjured up in the stories his grandmother tells him. Grandmother Charlotte came to Russia as a young nurse in the First World War, married a Russian lawyer and, when he died at the Front, never returned to her native land. Now living in a remote village on the edge of the Russian steppes, Charlotte welcomes the narrator, tellingly called Andrei, for long summer vacations at her house and there regales him with her tales of the glorious, half-fantastic country that she remembers from her own youth. His grandmother invokes in Andrei a love of the imagined beauties of France but he also possesses a deep, instinctive, almost perverse attachment to Russia. 'The more the Russia I was discovering revealed itself to be black,' he notes, 'the more this attachment became violent.' As Andrei grows older, he struggles to reconcile his two homelands. *Le Testament Français* is a powerful and lyrical coming-of-age story which explores the ways in which memory and imagination play their parts in the construction of personal identity.

🕮 Read on

Human Love; *The Woman Who Waited*
Milan Kundera, *Ignorance*

DAVID MALOUF (b. 1934) AUSTRALIA

REMEMBERING BABYLON (1993)

International IMPAC Dublin Literary Award 1996

David Malouf, one of the most admired Australian writers of his generation, has published poetry, volumes of short stories, idiosyncratic memoirs of his own life and ten novels. Some of his fiction has ranged far and wide in time and space (*An Imaginary Life*, for example, describes the exile of the Roman poet Ovid) but his most characteristic work explores, in prose of a rich and poetic range, the history of his native country. *The Conversations at Curlow Creek*, for example, is set in 1827 and takes the shape of a night-long conversation between Carney, an Irish bushranger who is to be hanged in the morning, and Adair, the police officer who is overseeing the hanging. As the two men talk, they discover that their past histories bring them closer together. *Remembering Babylon* is set in Queensland in the nineteenth century and tells the story of Gemmy, who suddenly appears out of the bush at the edge of a small white settlement. Gemmy is himself white but, after a shipwreck, he has spent sixteen years living with the Aborigines. All the white characters in the novel are alternately fascinated and appalled by Gemmy's ambiguous status, the position he holds poised between two, for them mutually exclusive, categories, white and black. Gemmy may be white but his years with the Aborigines have marked him. He hardly remembers any English and his sense of self and the natural world belong to his adopted people. As the novel progresses and Gemmy moves towards the realisation that, to save himself, he must return once more to the bush, one can only admire the skill with which Malouf unfolds his story. The very first winner of the prestigious and financially rewarding International IMPAC Dublin Literary Award, *Remembering Babylon* is a book that explores ideas of identity and colonialism with great subtlety and intelligence.

🦜 Read on

The Conversations at Curlow Creek; *An Imaginary Life*
≫ Peter Carey, *True History of the Kelly Gang*; Thomas Keneally, *The Chant of Jimmie Blacksmith*; Patrick White, *A Fringe of Leaves*

HILARY MANTEL (b. 1952) UK

WOLF HALL (2009)

Man Booker Prize 2009

Author of both historical and contemporary novels, Hilary Mantel is a writer who eludes pigeon-holing or easy definition. She has written books that examine inequalities of class, race and gender in South Africa (*A Change of Climate*) and in Saudi Arabia (*Eight Months on Ghazzah Street*). She has written a sweeping, rather old-fashioned novel about the French Revolution (*A Place of Greater Safety*) and a strange, haunting parable of religion and possible redemption (*Fludd*) that would not look too out of place in the collected works of Muriel Spark. However, her greatest popular success has come with her recent Man Booker Prize-winning novel entitled *Wolf Hall*, a large-scale and ambitious narrative, set in the court of Henry VIII and focusing on the rise to power of Thomas Cromwell. Mantel's Cromwell, right-hand man to Cardinal Wolsey in the earlier sections of her huge book, is a man of many parts – 'at home in courtroom or waterfront, bishop's palace or inn yard'. He is someone who 'can draft a contract, train a falcon, draw a map, stop a street fight, furnish a house and fix a jury'. He is also a much more sympathetic character than the Cromwell we usually meet in the history books. As Wolsey's star wanes, Cromwell's rises and his success in smoothing Henry VIII's path towards marriage with Anne Boleyn is rewarded with the king's confidence. His opposite number, so often portrayed as saint but here a cold and self-regarding bigot, is Thomas More. All the central figures (Wolsey, the king, Catherine of Aragon, a young Mary Tudor, the Boleyn sisters) from one of the most familiar periods in English history parade through Mantel's pages and she brings them all vividly to life. She seamlessly blends historical research with her own invention to produce a novel of great verve and vitality.

🐚 Read on

Beyond Black; *The Giant, O'Brien*; *A Place of Greater Safety*
▶▶ Helen Dunmore, *The Siege*; C.J. Sansom, *Dissolution*; ▶▶ Rose Tremain, *Restoration*

CORMAC McCARTHY (b. 1933) USA

THE ROAD (2006)

Pulitzer Prize for Fiction 2007

Cormac McCarthy began to publish his fiction in the 1960s and his unforgiving vision of America's past, present and future has made him one of his country's most admired living authors. Until recently, he was best known for *Blood Meridian*, a novel in which the American West is utterly divested of any mythology and romance and depicted as an inferno of violence, and for the so-called Border Trilogy (*All the Pretty Horses*, *The Crossing* and *Cities of the Plain*). Now, thanks to a superb film adaptation and the award of the Pulitzer Prize for Fiction, his most famous novel is probably *The Road*, a dark vision of a post-apocalyptic world in which a father and son struggle to survive in a blighted landscape. McCarthy never makes clear exactly what has happened but America has been ravaged by a terrible catastrophe. The land has become a burning wreck, where ash drifts permanently in the air and nothing can grow. The survivors of disaster have been reduced to an animal existence and, in the desperate search for food, many have turned to cannibalism. Through this ruined world the man and the boy are making their way towards the coast. They have nothing but the ragged clothes they wear, a trolley carrying their paltry belongings and a pistol to defend themselves against any marauders they might meet on the road. They have nothing to sustain them but their mutual love and the faint hope that things might be better at the coast than they are inland. McCarthy describes their journey in a pared-down prose of extraordinary power and beauty. His vision of a world from which nearly everything we value has been stripped is bleak in the extreme but, out of the very depths, he conjures up a small spark of humanity that shines all the brighter for the darkness in which it is placed.

🎬 **Film version:** *The Road* (2009)

📖 **Read on**
Blood Meridian; *All the Pretty Horses*; *No Country For Old Men*
Bernard Malamud, *God's Grace*; George R. Stewart, *Earth Abides*; Marianne Wiggins, *John Dollar*

READONATHEME: PULITZER PRIZE-WINNERS

The main entries in this book have been restricted to books that won prizes in the years after 1980. The Pulitzer Prize for the Novel was first awarded in 1918 and changed its name to the Pulitzer Prize for Fiction in 1948. Here is a list of just some of the books that won the Prize under either of its names in the years before 1980

Saul Bellow, *Humboldt's Gift* (1976)

Pearl S. Buck, *The Good Earth* (1932)

William Faulkner, *The Reivers* (1963)

Ernest Hemingway, *The Old Man and the Sea* (1953)

Harper Lee, *To Kill a Mockingbird* (1961)

Bernard Malamud, *The Fixer* (1967)

James A. Michener, *Tales of the South Pacific* (1948)

Margaret Mitchell, *Gone with the Wind* (1937)

Marjorie Kinnan Rawlings, *The Yearling* (1939)

John Steinbeck, *The Grapes of Wrath* (1940)

William Styron, *The Confessions of Nat Turner* (1968)

Robert Penn Warren, *All the King's Men* (1947)

Eudora Welty, *The Optimist's Daughter* (1973)

Edith Wharton, *The Age of Innocence* (1921)

Herman Wouk, *The Caine Mutiny* (1952)

IAN McEWAN (b. 1948) UK

ATONEMENT (2001)

W.H. Smith Literary Award 2002

Ian McEwan began his career in the 1970s writing short stories and short novels in which, in precise and glacially cool prose, he led his readers towards hidden horrors and terrible revelations. In the 1980s he moved on to longer narratives and he has since established himself as perhaps Britain's most widely admired literary novelist. His fiction has ranged from the story of a man whose comfortable middle-class life is arbitrarily disrupted by the obsessions and delusions of another man (*Enduring Love*) to a tender and ironic novella about a relationship ruined by repression and sexual inexperience (*On Chesil Beach*). *Atonement*, one of his finest works, is an extended drama in three acts. In the first it is 1935 and a teenage girl, Briony Tallis, fatefully misinterprets events around her. She watches, and half-understands, the sexual attraction between her older sister Cecilia and a Cambridge graduate Robbie Turner but half-understanding is not enough. Trusted as a go-between by the two would-be lovers, she allows the story she has constructed about what is happening to stand in the way of acknowledging what the reality is. The result is tragedy not only for Robbie and Cecilia but also, eventually, for herself. The other two parts of the book take place in 1940 and follow Robbie in the retreat to Dunkirk and Briony, striving to atone for her mistake and working as a probationary nurse in a Blitz-racked London. In a coda, set in 1999, Briony, now an old woman and a successful writer, looks back at her younger self, cleverly overturns our expectations and invites us to re-examine the 'atonement' she has presented to us. A shape-shifting narrative that rarely allows readers to be certain of where they stand, *Atonement* succeeds both as an exploration of guilt and reparation over sixty years and as a subtle demonstration of the powers of story-telling.

Film version: *Atonement* (2007, starring Keira Knightley as Cecilia and James McAvoy as Robbie)

Read on
Enduring Love; *On Chesil Beach*; *Saturday*
L.P. Hartley, *The Go-Between*; ›› Graham Swift, *Waterland*

JON McGREGOR (b. 1976)

IF NOBODY SPEAKS OF REMARKABLE THINGS
(2002)

Betty Trask Award 2003

In three novels published over the last eight years, Jon McGregor has established himself as one of the most exciting and original young novelists in Britain. His books zoom in on the lives of ordinary people and his prose has a remarkable ability to invest everyday life with a sense of the extraordinary. Little happens in the way of a conventional plot in his fiction. In his most recent book, *Even the Dogs*, he begins with a death but spends much of his time chronicling the daily struggles of a handful of addicts to survive on the streets of an anonymous Midlands city. In his debut novel, *If Nobody Speaks of Remarkable Things*, the narrative seems to do little but meander through the mundane activities of a group of people living on a suburban street until it arrives at the one major event in the book – a climactic accident that casts its shadow from the first pages but doesn't arrive until the last. But, in his apparent wanderings, McGregor brings to life his unexceptional, often unnamed, characters in ways that other, more overtly flamboyant novelists fail to do. The ageing war veteran who is trying to keep news of his fatal illness from his wife, the man whose hands are scarred from a domestic fire, the young man suffering from unrequited love for a neighbour to whom he has scarcely ever spoken – they are people that we might fail to notice if we passed them in the street but McGregor invites us to acknowledge their individuality and the hidden dramas of their lives. 'This is a very big world,' one character tells his young daughter, 'and there are many many things you could miss if you are not careful ... there are remarkable things all the time, right in front of us.' Jon McGregor's skill is in directing us towards paying attention to those remarkable things.

🐟 Read on

So Many Ways to Begin; *Even the Dogs*

>> David Mitchell, *Black Swan Green*; Ali Smith, *Hotel World*

JAMES MEEK (b. 1962) UK

THE PEOPLE'S ACT OF LOVE (2005)

Ondaatje Prize 2006

An award-winning journalist and foreign correspondent, James Meek has also published two collections of short stories and four novels. The most recent of the novels is *We Are Now Beginning Our Descent* which charts its central character's journey from Afghanistan to the American Deep South in pursuit of an intense love affair. The best of his fiction is undoubtedly *The People's Act of Love* which won the Ondaatje Prize the year after its publication. This prize is one that is given to books that evoke the spirit of a place. The place that is conjured up so vividly in Meek's novel is the bleak landscape of Siberia in 1919. The small township of Yazyk is under martial law but its rulers are not Russian. They are the survivors of a regiment of Czech soldiers, unwilling conscripts against the Bolsheviks, who have been stranded in the wastelands of the far north. Led by their deranged commander, Captain Matula, the Czechs terrorise the people of Yazyk, most of whom are members of a strange Christian sect, yet they long only to escape from their frozen exile. Into this trapped community comes a charismatic man called Samarin, claiming to be a revolutionary who has fled from one of the Tsar's gulags. His arrival triggers a sequence of violent events which engulf every character in the novel from Matula and Samarin himself to Lieutenant Mutz, a humane Czech officer plotting to escape Matula's megalomaniac tyranny, Balashov, the enigmatic leader of the sect, and Anna Petrovna, a young widow whose past contains disturbing secrets. At one level *The People's Act of Love* is a novel of war and adventure that grips the imagination from its opening pages. It is also an unflinching analysis of the ways in which utopian dreams spiral out of control and end as nightmares of oppression and inhumanity.

☙ Read on
We Are Now Beginning Our Descent
Ken Kalfus, *The Commissariat of Enlightenment*

ANNE MICHAELS (b. 1958) CANADA

FUGITIVE PIECES (1997)

Orange Prize 1997

Anne Michaels is a poet who has also written two novels. The most recent (published in 2008) is *The Winter Vault*, in which the rescue of the temples at Abu Simbel in Egypt from the waters of the new Aswan Dam in 1964 is the backdrop for the love, loss and grief experienced by a young engineer and his wife. Eleven years earlier, her first novel, *Fugitive Pieces* was the second winner of the Orange Prize. At the heart of Michaels's book is the story of Jakob Beer. At the beginning of the novel, Jakob is a small boy who has fled the Nazis and the scene of his parents' murder and is in hiding in the dark forests of Poland. Covered in mud and filth, he is discovered by Athos Roussos, a Greek scholar who is excavating the ancient Polish city of Biskupin. Athos takes responsibility for the boy and smuggles him out of Poland and back to his home on the Greek island of Zakynthos. As Jakob grows up, Athos becomes his beloved mentor, who introduces him to the pleasures of knowledge and language and intellectual curiosity but the young man remains haunted by his loss and, especially, by fleeting memories of a sister whose final fate he has never learned. The narrative continues to follow Jakob as he moves from Europe to Canada and back again, charting the failure of his marriage, his attempts to come to terms with his extraordinary past and his short-lived happiness with a much younger woman. Charged with the lyrical and evocative language of a poet, *Fugitive Pieces* is a book to read and re-read. As one reviewer wrote at the time of its first publication, 'All except a handful of contemporary novels are dwarfed by its reach, its compassion and its wisdom.'

 Film version: *Fugitive Pieces* (2007, with Stephen Dillane as Jakob Beer)

Read on

The Winter Vault

Bernhard Schlink, *The Reader*; Rachel Seiffert, *The Dark Room*

ANDREW MILLER (b. 1960) UK

INGENIOUS PAIN (1997)

International IMPAC Dublin Literary Award 1999

Amongst those shortlisted for the International IMPAC Dublin Literary Award in 1999 were such world-renowned writers as Don DeLillo, Haruki Murakami and >> Ian McEwan. In the event, the prize was won by a debut English novelist in his thirties named Andrew Miller. His book, *Ingenious Pain*, is set in the eighteenth century and its central character is James Dyer, a man born with a freakish inability to feel pain and love. After a picaresque progress through life, he ends up as a successful surgeon. While travelling to Russia to treat the Empress Catherine the Great, Dyer encounters a witch-woman with supernatural powers whose gift of a 'heart' finally introduces him to the difficult realities of human emotions and the world of feeling. Half carefully researched historical novel and half excursion into the difficult territory of magic realism, *Ingenious Pain* was an intriguing and imaginative winner of what is the most valuable monetary prize presented for a single work of fiction published in English. Miller followed this unsettling first novel with *Casanova*, another historical novel set in the eighteenth century, in which the legendary seducer, exiled from his home city of Venice, arrives in London and embarks on a doomed and obsessive love affair. In later fiction he has moved seamlessly from the Age of Reason to the twentieth century. *Oxygen*, for example, tells the story of two sons who gather at their mother's deathbed. One is a fading actor reduced to auditioning for porn movies, the other a literary translator working on a play by a famous Hungarian writer. The book moves between the lives of the two brothers and that of the playwright, still haunted by his experiences in the 1956 Hungarian Uprising, as it explores the meaning of love, courage and redemption. *Oxygen* was shortlisted for both the Booker Prize and the Whitbread Prize. It won neither but it seems certain that it is only a matter of time before Miller's fiction again catches the eye of the judges of a major award.

🕮 Read on

Casanova; *Oxygen*; *One Morning Like a Bird*
Ross King, *Domino*; Patrick Suskind, *Perfume*

STEVEN MILLHAUSER (b. 1943) USA

MARTIN DRESSLER: THE TALE OF AN AMERICAN DREAMER (1996)

Pulitzer Prize for Fiction 1997

Millhauser's first novel was *Edwin Mulhouse*, a witty and tongue-in-cheek story of a novelist and child prodigy who dies at the age of only eleven, and he went on to produce several other novels and collections of short stories which demonstrated a similar offbeat inventiveness and imagination. His greatest success has been the Pulitzer Prize-winning *Martin Dressler*. On one level, this begins as a meticulously researched historical novel, set in late nineteenth-century New York, which traces the rise of its eponymous hero from bellboy to the greatest hotelier in the city. 'There once lived a man named Martin Dressler,' it opens, 'a shopkeeper's son, who rose from modest beginnings to a height of dreamlike good fortune.' Yet, as this first line suggests, Millhauser's story is also one that is going to resemble a fairy story in which an impoverished hero wins through to riches and success. In the earlier part of the book it is the historical novel that takes precedence but, as the narrative progresses and Dressler the entrepreneur imagines ever more elaborate palaces of pleasure for his guests, the fairy tale elements come to the fore. By the time his central character builds his greatest hotel, the Grand Cosmo, 'a world within the world, rivalling that world', Millhauser has left realism far behind him. One floor of the hotel appears to be wooded countryside; another is shaped like mountains and the bedrooms are luxuriously appointed caverns. Guests stroll beneath artificial moonlight or visit a Temple of Poesy. Dressler has brought his dreams to life and yet the Grand Cosmo proves a failure. He is forced to confess to himself that, 'he had dreamed the wrong dream, the dream that others didn't wish to enter'. In describing the rise and fall of his extravagant dreamer, Millhauser has written his own brilliantly ironic version of the classic American tale of rags to riches.

≋ Read on

Edwin Mulhouse; *The Barnum Museum* (short stories)
Reif Larsen, *The Selected Works of T.S. Spivet*; George Saunders, *CivilWarLand in Bad Decline*

DAVID MITCHELL (b. 1969) UK

GHOSTWRITTEN (1999)

John Llewellyn Rhys Prize 1999

From the very outset of his career, David Mitchell has shown a determination to stray away from the paths of traditional linear narrative. In his very first novel, *Ghostwritten*, characters hand on the narrative baton as stories blossom and multiply. The novel opens with a section that focuses on a man calling himself Quasar, a member of a cult which has launched a gas attack on the Tokyo Underground, who has fled to Okinawa to avoid arrest. The next section is set in Tokyo where a teenage jazz buff named Satoru has a chance encounter with a girl from Hong Kong; the two become peripheral characters in the novel's next section as a dodgy English lawyer named Neal Brose working in Hong Kong is forced to deal with complications in his personal and professional lives. The novel moves on to a holy mountain in China, to Mongolia, St. Petersburg and London before coming full circle and returning to Japan and the terrorist attack involving Quasar. As the narrative travels around the world, Mitchell creates a weirdly varied and intriguing cast of characters whose stories constantly interlink and cross-reference with one another. He followed *Ghostwritten* with two equally experimental works in *number9dream* and *Cloud Atlas*. His more recent fiction has been less dazzlingly different in its narrative techniques. *Black Swan Green* tells a much simpler story than his earlier books of an adolescent boy growing up in a sleepy village in Worcestershire in the 1980s; *The Thousand Autumns of Jacob de Zoet*, although epic in its ambitions, is, by Mitchell's standards, a comparatively conventional work of historical fiction set in an eighteenth-century trading *entrepôt* between East and West. Whatever he has written over the last decade, this remarkable author has proved himself to be one of the great virtuosos of modern world fiction.

🐚 Read on

Cloud Atlas; *Black Swan Green*; *The Thousand Autumns of Jacob de Zoet*

Paul Auster, *The Music of Chance*; Haruki Murakami, *The Wind-Up Bird Chronicle*

TIMOTHY MO (b. 1950) UK

SOUR SWEET (1982)

Hawthornden Prize 1982

Born in Hong Kong to an English mother and a Chinese father, Timothy Mo moved to England with his family when he was ten years old. He went on to study history at St. John's College, Oxford and, after graduating, he worked as a journalist on a variety of magazines, including the *Times Education Supplement*, *New Statesman* and *Boxing News*, before publishing his first novel *The Monkey King*, a wry comedy of manners set in post-war Hong Kong, in 1978. Mo's second novel, *Sour Sweet* not only won the Hawthornden Prize but was also short-listed for the Booker Prize. It is an ironic tale of cultural mis-understandings which takes as its subject the plight of a Chinese immigrant family struggling to make a living in London during the 1960s. Chen, his wife Lily, young son Man Kee and his wife's sister Mui live in NW9. Chen initially works in a Chinese restaurant in Soho but is later persuaded to open one of his own in the furthest reaches of South London. As his business succeeds, it inevitably attracts the attentions of the triad gangs which still possess power in the Chinese community. Chen must find his own ways of accommodation with the triads. In the decades since he wrote *Sour Sweet*, Timothy Mo has published only four further novels, two of them under a publishing imprint which he founded himself. All have turned away from the smaller dramas of his first two novels and addressed much larger and more epic themes – *An Insular Possession*, for example, is an ambitious historical novel set at the time of the nineteenth-century Opium Wars between Britain and China. His later fiction has not been without its many admirers (and *Renegade or Halo2* won the James Tait Black Memorial Prize) but there is an argument to be made that he has never written with such precision and insight as he did in *Sour Sweet*.

 Film version: *Soursweet* (1988)

 Read on

An Insular Possession; *The Monkey King*

›› Hanif Kureishi, *The Black Album*; **››** John Lanchester, *Fragrant Harbour*

LAWRENCE NORFOLK (b. 1963) UK

LEMPRIERE'S DICTIONARY (1991)

Somerset Maugham Award 1992

Lawrence Norfolk won a place on the 1993 *Granta* list of Best Young British Novelists solely on the strength of **Lemprière's Dictionary**, published two years before the list was announced. Superficially, this first novel is the story of the eighteenth-century scholar John Lemprière, author of a dictionary of classical literature and the classical world that was, for a long time, a standard work. However, Norfolk creates an imaginary life for Lemprière, blending historical reality, classical allusions, fantasy and improbable conspiracy theories into a huge fictional extravaganza. Stories from ancient mythology jostle for the reader's attention with rich evocations of the street life of Georgian London; Lemprière's Huguenot ancestry is shown to have strange connections with the rise to wealth and power of the East India Company; pirates, plotters, assassins and revolutionaries stalk the book's pages. Like an English version of Umberto Eco, Norfolk crams his story with the fruits of his wide reading and examples of his improbable erudition. The result is a book that seems always on the verge of breaking down the barrier between history and fiction and justifying the remark attributed to its author in several interviews that everything that appears plausible in it is invented and everything that seems unlikely is historically accurate. Lawrence Norfolk has gone on to publish two further novels. **The Pope's Rhinoceros** is another work of historical fiction, this time set in the sixteenth century, which builds a startling edifice of stories on the foundations of a quest for a rhinoceros, an almost mythical beast at the time, to deliver to Pope Leo X; *In the Shape of a Boar* begins with Norfolk's re-telling of a story from Greek mythology and moves forward to the Second World War and events which echo it. Both confirm his status as one of the most restlessly inventive and original British novelists of his generation.

🔖 Read on

The Pope's Rhinoceros; *In the Shape of a Boar*
Andrew Davidson, *The Gargoyle*; ❯❯ Umberto Eco, *Baudolino*; Neal Stephenson, *Quicksilver*

JOSEPH O'NEILL (b. 1964) IRELAND/USA

NETHERLAND (2008)

PEN/Faulkner Award for Fiction 2009

Any work of fiction that can combine the effects of 9/11 on New York, cricket and echoes of F. Scott Fitzgerald's classic novel *The Great Gatsby* into one narrative has to be a book worth reading and *Netherland* is certainly that. Its narrator is a Dutch stockbroker named Hans van den Broek, left in New York when his English wife and their small son travel back to London in the aftermath of the attack on the Twin Towers. Hans was once a lover of cricket and, in his new and uncomfortable loneliness, living on his own in the Chelsea Hotel, he learns that there are cricketers even in New York. He begins to play the game again with a team of expatriates and immigrants and meets a charismatic man from the West Indies named Chuck Ramkissoon. Just as Nick Carraway was drawn to the enigmatic Jay Gatsby in Fitzgerald's novel, so Hans becomes fascinated by his new friend. Chuck is a man of dreams and ambitions. He plans to build a cricket stadium in Brooklyn, he tells Hans, and turn the game into a major American spectator sport. The Dutchman is both amused and intrigued by the West Indian but, as he spends more time with him, he realises that there is a dark side to Chuck. He is heavily involved in gambling rackets and gangsterism. The friendship, which began with a shared love of cricket, is ultimately doomed by the difference between the two worlds the men inhabit. Told in retrospect by Hans, now living again in London, after he hears the news that Chuck's murdered body has been found at the bottom of a New York canal, *Netherland* is a haunting book about love and friendship, about the sense of belonging and not belonging and about the darker underside of the American dream.

📖 Read on

The Breezes; *This is the Life* (O'Neill's two previous novels)
Colum McCann, *This Side of Brightness*

MICHAEL ONDAATJE (b. 1943) SRI LANKA/CANADA

ANIL'S GHOST (2000)

Governor General's Literary Award for Fiction 2000

Born in Sri Lanka, Michael Ondaatje spent his childhood there and in England and then moved to Canada as a young man. After studying in Toronto and Kingston, Ontario, he became a university lecturer in English literature and a poet. When he started to write fiction, it was in a prose that was as rich, dense and allusive as his verse. Early, experimental novels like *Coming Through Slaughter* and *The Collected Works of Billy the Kid* won him admirers but it was only with the publication of *The English Patient*, the story of an enigmatic casualty of the Second World War, which won the Booker Prize and was later transformed by Anthony Minghella into a successful film, that Ondaatje gained a much wider audience. *Anil's Ghost* was Ondaatje's first novel after *The English Patient* and focuses on Anil Tissera, a Western-educated forensic anthropologist, who is drawn into the troubled politics of her native Sri Lanka when she begins a quest for the identity of a modern skeleton found on an ancient archaeological site. Anil has been away from Sri Lanka for many years and she finds herself treading warily through the dangerous minefield of a society she no longer fully understands. How far can she trust her colleague Sarath? How difficult and dangerous would it be if the skeleton, which they nickname Sailor, was to be identified as a victim of atrocities in the recent civil war? What ghosts still haunt Sri Lanka and its people? Anil's dilemmas are only made worse when Sailor disappears. Moving backwards and forwards in time between the present (sometime in the

1990s) and the past lives of its central characters, *Anil's Ghost* is a book which uses some of the themes and motifs of the forensic thriller to tell a riveting story of a country harrowed by a civil war and its dark legacy.

❧ Read on

Divisadero; *The English Patient* (Ondaatje's earlier, major success which won both the Booker Prize and the Canadian Governor-General's Literary Award)
Amitav Ghosh, *The Hungry Tide*; Romesh Gunesekera, *Reef*

ORHAN PAMUK (b. 1952) TURKEY

MY NAME IS RED (1998)

International IMPAC Dublin Literary Award 2003

Orhan Pamuk, who won the Nobel Prize for Literature in 2006, has spent much of his life in Istanbul and the city has shaped his imagination. One of the best introductions to his work may well be *Istanbul: Memories of a City*, a digressive memoir of his childhood and adolescence which is also an evocative tribute to the place of his birth. His fiction has ranged from *Snow*, the story of an exiled poet returning to Turkey and travelling to the remote city of Kars on the Russian border, to *The New Life*, a haunting fantasy of a man who grows obsessed by the magical powers of a book. However, his finest novels draw on the history which haunts his later memoir. *The White Castle*, for example, is set in the seventeenth century and traces the relationship between two scholars, one a Turkish savant living in Constantinople, the other a Venetian captured and sold to him as a slave. *My Name Is Red* is arguably Pamuk's masterpiece. In this complex and subtle novel a miniaturist, engaged to produce a magnificently illuminated book for a sixteenth-century Sultan, is murdered. This becomes the starting point for a narrative that is partly a kind of detective story and partly an investigation into the interconnections between love and art and power. The artists who work on the Sultan's book are not only caught up in the mystery of who killed their colleague. They are also at the heart of a debate about the nature of art itself – should it continue to follow the ancient traditions of the East or adopt the new techniques of the West? – and they are threatened by the Machiavellian plotting and jostling for position that surrounds the ruler. Using short chapters and a miscellany of often unlikely narrators, Pamuk creates an extraordinarily original portrait of a past culture.

🕮 Read on

The New Life; *Snow*; *The White Castle*
Ismail Kadare, *The Siege*; Amin Maalouf, *Balthasar's Odyssey*

STEF PENNEY (b. 1969) UK

THE TENDERNESS OF WOLVES (2006)

Costa Book of the Year 2006

Stef Penney's atmospheric murder mystery set in the icy wastes of northern Canada during the 1860s was a first novel but it won immediate acclaim from the reviewers, was voted Costa Book of the Year and went on to become a bestseller worldwide. A minor controversy was aroused when it was revealed that Penney, an Edinburgh-born film-maker, had never visited Canada before the book was published and had done all her research for it in the British Library. How, some people asked, could the novel be deemed properly authentic? Others, more attuned to the power of the imagination, pointed out that Penney had never visited the 1860s either but had still succeeded in recreating the era convincingly for her narrative. *The Tenderness of Wolves* opens with the discovery of a brutal murder in the small Canadian settlement of Dove River. The fur trader, Laurent Jammet, is found in his cabin with his throat slit and his hair scalped. Suspicion falls on the seventeen-year-old Francis Ross, an unhappy loner, alienated from his own family, who disappears at the time of the killing. A trail leads northwards into the wilderness and Francis's adoptive mother joins forces with a taciturn tracker named Parker, himself a suspect in the murder, and Donald Moody, a naive young employee of the Hudson's Bay Company, to follow it. Out in the wilds they come across first a strange religious community seeking to live a holy life away from the temptations of civilisation and then an isolated, half-forgotten trading outpost ruled over by a disturbing figure from

Parker's past. As the novel reaches its climax in a bloody confrontation between those responsible for Jammet's death and their pursuers, Penney brings together all the varying threads of her plot and weaves them into a memorable and highly satisfying conclusion.

🕮 Read on

Gil Adamson, *The Outlander*; ›› Guy Vanderhaeghe, *The Last Crossing*

PER PETTERSON (b. 1952) NORWAY

OUT STEALING HORSES (2003)

International IMPAC Dublin Literary Award 2007

Per Petterson has long had a high reputation as a novelist in his native Norway. *To Siberia*, a story set as the world teeters on the brink of the Second World War, and *In the Wake*, a potent study of a man wrestling with terrible grief and loss, won much acclaim when they were first published. However, winning the International IMPAC Dublin Literary Award for *Out Stealing Horses*, a stark but compellingly written story of an elderly man recalling the events of a long-ago summer in the country, brought him to the attention of a worldwide readership. Trond Sander is in his late sixties and has moved to a remote wooden house in the far east of Norway after the death of his wife in a car crash. 'All my life I have longed to be alone in a place like this,' he notes and he is happy at first to have found the solitude he has desired. His isolation is disturbed by a meeting with his nearest neighbour which sends him back in time fifty years to a period spent with his beloved father in a cabin in the forest. Trond's companion then was another fifteen-year-old boy named Jon and the old man now recalls the long-vanished day when Jon came calling with an invitation to go 'out stealing horses'. That day began as an exhilarating boyhood adventure and ended with Trond's realisation that something terrible had happened in his friend's life. One of his younger, twin brothers had accidentally shot and killed the other. This is but the first of a series of revelations that summer which rock Trond's sense of himself and others. In spare and unpretentious prose, Per Petterson creates a seemingly simple story of grief and loss and memory which none the less lingers long in the mind once it is finished.

≋ Read on

In the Wake; *To Siberia*
Peter Høeg, *Miss Smilla's Feeling for Snow*

CARYL PHILLIPS (b. 1958) UK

CROSSING THE RIVER (1993)

James Tait Black Memorial Prize 1993

One of the major concerns of Caryl Phillips's fiction is the dark legacy of colonialism and his novels often feature characters who struggle directly with the crises of identity that it can engender. It is true of an early novel such as *Cambridge* which uses two very different narrative voices to tell a chilling tale of a West Indian island society irredeemably tainted by the inhumanity on which it is built. It is true, more indirectly of *Foreigners*, a more recent volume of three novellas about three black Englishmen alienated by their experiences of racism. And it is certainly true of his prize-winning 1993 novel, *Crossing the River*. 'I sold my beloved children' is among the book's opening lines and the complex, intertwining but brilliantly handled narratives that follow show how the consequences of that transaction between a destitute African father and the English master of a slave ship reverberate through two hundred years of oppression and alienation. In three stories set at three different periods of history, characters who remain, in some sense, the 'children' of that original transaction struggle with its legacy. An emancipated slave sent to Liberia in the 1830s is unable to reconcile the warring elements within himself of the Christianity to which he subscribes and the Africa which he experiences; a black woman freed after the American Civil War journeys westwards in search of the husband and daughter she lost in the slave years; during World War II, an English-woman, victim of an abusive marriage, finds solace in an affair with a black GI. A fourth narrative, in some ways the most daring of them all, contrasts the blank amorality of a slave-ship captain in his 'business' with the passion and love he expresses in his letters to his wife. The four separate tales combine to produce a moving, multi-faceted picture of the human consequences of the forced diaspora from Africa.

🕮 Read on

Cambridge; *The Nature of Blood*
Fred D'Aguiar, *Feeding the Ghosts*; David Dabydeen, *The Counting House*

ANNIE PROULX (b. 1935) USA

THE SHIPPING NEWS (1993)

Pulitzer Prize for Fiction 1994

Annie Proulx did not begin to publish her fiction until she was in her fifties but her original (often dark) imagination, her evocative use of landscape and setting, her quirky humour and arresting use of language were apparent both in *Heart Songs*, a collection of short stories published in 1988 and in her first novel, *Postcards*, the tragic saga of an American farming family, which followed four years later. Later fiction, such as *Accordion Crimes*, which uses a sequence of interconnected tales about a button accordion and the different people who own it to build up a rich picture of the immigrant experience in the USA, was similarly imaginative. Today she may well be best known as the author of the novella, 'Brokeback Mountain', in which two Wyoming ranch-hands are drawn into an intense sexual relationship and struggle to accommodate this desire within their macho sense of self. The story became a successful film starring Heath Ledger and Jake Gyllenhaal. Before the triumph of Ang Lee's movie, Proulx's most familiar work was her second novel, *The Shipping News*. This was exceptionally well reviewed and went on to win the Pulitzer Prize for Fiction the year after it appeared. At the beginning of the book, its central character Quoyle is an unsuccessful newspaperman in New York, still brooding on the humiliations of his marriage to a woman who first betrayed him and then was killed in an accident, leaving him with two small children. Accompanied by his young daughters and by a formidable maiden aunt, he returns to Newfoundland, his father's birthplace, and there he finds the fulfilment that eluded him in the city. He establishes himself at the local newspaper, finds himself drawn into the daily life of the community and emerges from the protective shell of loneliness to begin a new and rewarding relationship. Quoyle's transformation becomes an offbeat celebration of the potential people have for change.

🎞 **Film version:** *The Shipping News* (2001, starring Kevin Spacey as Quoyle)

📖 **Read on**
Accordion Crimes; *Close Range* (the collection of stories which includes 'Brokeback Mountain')
Richard Ford, *The Sportswriter*; Elizabeth McCracken, *The Giant's House*

ROSS RAISIN (b. 1979) UK
GOD'S OWN COUNTRY (2008)

Betty Trask Award 2008

It's not every debut novelist who can use a quote from a Nobel Prize-winner to adorn the dustjacket of his first book but Ross Raisin's *God's Own Country* was praised by no less a figure than J.M. Coetzee who called it 'chilling in its effect and convincing in its execution'. Certainly the voice of its narrator, funny and unsettling at the same time, lodges itself in the reader's mind from the opening few lines. 'Ramblers. Daft sods in pink and green hats. It wasn't even cold. They moved down the field, swing-swaying like a line of drunks, addled with the air and the land, and the smell of manure.' The voice belongs to Sam Marsdyke, a young and gangling misfit who works for his father on his isolated hill farm in North Yorkshire. Expelled from school after what might or might not have been a sexual assault on a fellow pupil, he spends much of his time trudging the hills and brooding on the frustrations and indignities of his life. His interest is aroused by the arrival of a family of 'towns', as he calls them, at a neighbouring farm. Amongst the family is a teenage girl. Over the following weeks and months, she becomes his obsession. Sam is awkward and taciturn in company but his inner life is one of fantasy and imagination and there the girl takes centre stage. She is lonely herself, exiled from the world she has previously known, and unwittingly she encourages Sam in his delusions. She aids him in a plot to rescue a puppy that his father has sold. She confides in him her own unhappiness and her plans of escape. When the two abscond across the moors, the narrative begins to move implacably towards tragedy. The skill and subtlety with which Raisin unfolds his tale suggest that Coetzee was entirely correct in marking him out as a writer to watch.

🦑 Read on

Edward Hogan, *Blackmoor*; Patrick McCabe, *The Butcher Boy*

MICHÈLE ROBERTS (b. 1949) UK

DAUGHTERS OF THE HOUSE (1992)

W.H. Smith Literary Award 1993

Michèle Roberts is often described as a feminist novelist and her novels deal with themes that can be seen as particularly feminist – female sexuality, the narrow bounds within which male society can limit femininity, religion's definitions of womanhood and the often troubling bonds that link mothers and daughters – but they resist easy pigeon-holing, as all good novels do. She can write a dazzling fantasy in which a woman visiting Venice transforms herself in her dreams into the Arkivist of the Ark, voyaging on the waters with five storytelling Sibyls (*The Book of Mrs Noah*) or a gospel according to Mary Magdalene (*The Wild Girl*). She can also produce fiction in which past and present stories intertwine such as *The Mistressclass* which links a contemporary narrative of sibling rivalry and betrayal with a recreation of Charlotte Bronte's relationship with the Belgian teacher Constantin Heger. *Daughters of the House*, which was shortlisted for the Booker Prize as well as winning the W.H. Smith award, is the story of two cousins, Thérèse and Léonie, growing up in a small Normandy village in the 1950s. A religious vision – embraced by Thérèse, eventually rejected by Léonie – shapes their adolescences as does the wartime secret harboured by their elders. The decades pass and secrets from the past emerge when the cousins are re-united after a long estrangement. Thérèse, who has chosen to live a life of seclusion as a nun, returns to the family estate where Léonie, now married to a local farmer and the mother of children, still lives. As the book weaves through a complex plot towards a revelation of what ties still bind the two of them so tightly, the dark consequences of wartime collaboration and the capture and murder of three Jews continue to flicker beneath the surface of their lives.

🐘 Read on

Fair Exchange; *The Mistressclass*
>> Margaret Atwood, *Cat's Eye*; Margaret Forster, *The Memory Box*; Jane Rogers, *Promised Lands*

JAMES ROBERTSON (b. 1958) UK

JOSEPH KNIGHT (2003)

Saltire Society Scottish Book of the Year 2003

Poet, short-story writer, author of children's books in Scots and founder of a Scots-language publisher, James Robertson has played a significant role in Scottish literature over the last twenty years. His first novel, *The Fanatic*, in which a man employed as a ghost in tours of historic Edinburgh is drawn into the past by his researches into the religious extremism of the seventeenth century, was published in 2000. A later novel, *The Testament of Gideon Mack*, was like an update of the Scottish classic, James Hogg's *The Confessions of a Justified Sinner*, in its story of a man who comes to believe that he has met the Devil.

Sandwiched between these two books, but no less impressive a work of fiction than either of them, came *Joseph Knight*. Robertson's second novel is based on the true story of an eighteenth-century slave sold to a Scotsman in Jamaica and then brought back to Scotland, where he took his master to law and disputed his status as a slave in Scottish law. After the defeat of the Young Pretender's army at Culloden, John Wedderburn is exiled to the West Indies. Exile turns out to be the making of him and he becomes a wealthy plantation owner. He also acquires slaves, among them the eponymous Joseph Knight. Wedderburn appears to be an enlightened slave owner (if that is not a contradiction in terms) but, when he returns home to Scotland with Knight and the black man absconds, his wrath is aroused. To him, Knight is his property in the same way as his house or his plantation and, over a period of more than twenty years, he pursues his claims over him. Cleverly exploring ideas of race, imperialism and the nature of human liberty within the context of a gripping historical narrative, James Robertson produces a novel of great power and conviction.

🕮 Read on

The Fanatic; *The Testament of Gideon Mack*

David Dabydeen, *A Harlot's Progress*; Douglas Galbraith, *The Rising Sun*

MARILYNNE ROBINSON (b. 1943) USA

HOUSEKEEPING (1980)

Hemingway Foundation/PEN Award 1982

In 1980, Marilynne Robinson published her first novel, *Housekeeping*, the story of two sisters and their eccentric upbringing in a small Midwestern town. Critics were enthralled by the carefully constructed cadences of its poetic prose and by its reworking of familiar motifs in American literature to tell an exclusively female coming-of-age story. The story takes place in the fictional community of Fingerbone, up in the mountains of Idaho, a place that, in Robinson's characteristically memorable words, has been 'chastened by an outsized landscape and extravagant weather, and chastened again by an awareness that the whole of human history had occurred elsewhere'. Here the narrator Ruth and her younger sister Lucille grow up. Their father has deserted them and their mother first delivers them to the porch of their grandmother's house and then commits suicide by driving her car into a nearby lake. The girls spend their childhood under the care of a succession of variously eccentric female relatives. The last and the most offbeat of these is their Aunt Sylvie. 'I have observed that, in the way people are strange, they grow stranger,' Ruth notes and this certainly true of Aunt Sylvie. She proves too strange for Lucille who wastes no time in moving out when she can but Ruth and her aunt continue in their own odd housekeeping together. In the thirty years since her much-acclaimed debut, Marilynne Robinson has published only two further novels. *Gilead*, narrated by an elderly preacher named John Ames, records the return of Ames's godson, the scapegrace Jack

Boughton, to the small Iowa town that gives the book its title and the sequence of events that this triggers. In *Home*, perspectives shift and we see some of the same events recorded in *Gilead* as they look to Jack Boughton and to his sister, Glory. In all three of her novels, Marilynne Robinson has revealed a distinctive fictional voice unlike any other in modern American literature.

Film version: *Housekeeping* (1987, directed by Bill Forsyth)

Read on
Gilead; *Home*
Paula Fox, *Desperate Characters*; Jane Smiley, *A Thousand Acres*

JED RUBENFELD (b. 1959) USA
THE INTERPRETATION OF MURDER (2006)
Richard and Judy Best Read of the Year 2007

This clever and compelling work of crime fiction, which imagines Freud and Jung involved in a murder mystery during their 1909 trip to America, was a first novel. Its author, Jed Rubenfeld, is a professor of Law at Yale and his earlier books were scholarly works on American constitutional law but, from the very opening pages of *The Interpretation of Murder*, readers can feel confident that they are in the hands of an exceptionally skilful storyteller. The novel's narrator is Dr. Stratham Younger, an early admirer of Freud's work who is waiting 'in the swelter and mob of Hoboken Harbour' to greet the Viennese master when the steamship carrying him from Europe docks there. Soon after Freud arrives in the city two crimes are committed which trouble and baffle the authorities. A wealthy debutante is found bound, whipped and strangled in a penthouse apartment above Broadway. The following night another young heiress named Nora Acton nearly meets a similar fate. She is discovered, wounded and traumatised, in her parents' house but is unable to tell anyone what has happened to her. The case seems tailor-made for Freud's theories about the recovery of repressed memories and the great man is enlisted to help in the search for Nora's assailant. He and his New York disciple set about the task but they soon discover that little about the attacks is what it seems. Jed Rubenfeld has recently published *The Death Instinct*, a second novel about Stratham Younger, which is set a decade later and takes his character from New York to Vienna and to another encounter with Freud. If it is anything like as good as its predecessor, readers are in for a treat. *The Interpretation of Murder* takes real-life events surrounding Freud's first (and only) visit to America and mixes them with his own inventions to produce a wonderfully engaging murder mystery.

≋ Read on

The Death Instinct
Caleb Carr, *The Alienist*; Matthew Pearl, *The Dante Club*; Frank Tallis, *Mortal Mischief*

SALMAN RUSHDIE (b. 1947) INDIA/UK

MIDNIGHT'S CHILDREN (1981)

Booker Prize 1981

Amidst all the drama surrounding the *fatwa* issued against his life after the publication of **The Satanic Verses** and his years spent under police protection, it often seemed to be forgotten that Salman Rushdie was not just a name regularly in the headlines but also a writer of exceptional brilliance. His work seemed to get lost in the controversy. Yet his second novel, **Midnight's Children**, is undoubtedly a masterpiece and has been recognised as such by those who sit on the judgement panels for literary prizes. Not only did it win the Booker Prize in the year that it was published, it also triumphed in a poll to identify the 'Booker of Bookers' – the finest novel of all those to win the prize in the first forty years of its existence. The story of **Midnight's Children**, endlessly inventive in the ways it unfolds, is told by Saleem Sinai, a worker in a Bombay pickle factory, relating to his lover Padma the saga of his own life, which also proves to be a reflection of the history of India and Pakistan in the decades before and since independence. By virtue of his role as one of midnight's children – those born at the exact hour India gained its independence from Britain – Saleem's fortunes and those of his country are inextricably intertwined. His narrative, mixing techniques that echo those of fictional forms as diverse as Hollywood and Bollywood movies, European novels like Grass's **The Tin Drum**, South American magic realism and the folk-tales of India, moves back and forth in time. Much of Rushdie's later fiction, from **The Moor's Last Sigh**, a hypnotic family saga, covering the lives of a Bombay dynasty over a period of more than a century, to *The Ground Beneath Her Feet* which boldly mixes the mythologies of East and West with the modern iconography of rock in its story of two superstar musicians, has been remarkable enough. But *Midnight's Children* retains its position as one of the most original and compelling novels of the last century.

≋ Read on

The Ground Beneath Her Feet; *The Moor's Last Sigh*; *Shame*
Günter Grass, *The Tin Drum*; Arundhati Roy, *The God of Small Things*

RICHARD RUSSO (b. 1949) USA

EMPIRE FALLS (2001)

Pulitzer Prize for Fiction 2002

Since the appearance of his first novel, *Mohawk*, in 1986, Richard Russo has published another half dozen and has gained a reputation as a witty and humane chronicler of the lives of ordinary small-town Americans. His most recent book, *That Old Cape Magic*, follows a year in the life of a film studies lecturer named Jack Griffin who has to be cast out of his comfort zone before he can have any hope of surviving his mid-life crisis. Russo's best-known work, and the one that won him the Pulitzer Prize, is *Empire Falls*. The novel is set in the small town in New England which provides it with a title. Empire Falls is a once-thriving, now struggling community whose history is entwined with the rise and fall of the textile mills that brought it prosperity and with the fortunes of the Whiting family who owned most of them. The Whitings, in the shape of the ageing matriarch Francine, still rule the roost from their family mansion on the edge of town but Empire Falls is now a town in steep decline. Miles Roby is the amiable but undynamic manager of the Empire Grill, an eating house owned by Francine who has promised the business to him when she dies but shows little sign that she is likely to do so in the near future. Miles has secret plans to open a competing restaurant but he has troubles in plenty to distract him from them. His wife is divorcing him, his daughter is struggling at high school and his brother, potential partner in his bid to escape the clutches of Francine, is suspected of dealing in dope. As Miles grapples with the assorted blows that fate deals him, Russo turns a compassionate eye both on him and on the people who share his life in Empire Falls.

🎞 **Film version:** *Empire Falls* (2005, TV mini-series, starring Ed Harris and Paul Newman)

📚 **Read on**
Bridge of Sighs; *That Old Cape Magic*
Richard Ford, *The Sportswriter*; ❯❯ Anne Tyler, *Dinner at the Homesick Restaurant*

ALICE SEBOLD (b. 1963) USA

THE LOVELY BONES (2002)

Richard and Judy Best Read of the Year 2004

'My name was Salmon, like the fish; first name, Susie. I was fourteen when I was murdered on December 6 1973 ... My murderer was a man from our neighbourhood. My mother liked his border flowers and my father talked to him once about fertilizer.' These are among the arresting opening lines of Alice Sebold's first novel, a story which is told by its posthumous young narrator as she looks down to watch over her sorrowing family and friends, her killer and the detective trying to solve the mystery of her death. Stranded in an interim heaven that she cannot leave until she has let go of her earthly concerns, Susie witnesses the effects of her rape and murder on those left behind. Her father copes with his grief by throwing himself into the search for the killer, persisting in his belief that he can be found long after the police have given up hope. Her mother retreats from the family and 'escapes her ruined heart in merciful adultery'. Her younger siblings deal with her absence as they grow older as best they can. Over the years, as Susie watches from her ambiguous afterlife, they do not forget her but they begin eventually to heal. The premise of Sebold's novel is such that the result might have been sickly kitsch but the story is anything but sentimental. Partly this is because the voice she creates for her dead teenager carries such conviction. Partly it is because Sebold, whose first book, *Lucky*, was a non-fiction account of her own traumatic experience, her rape when a student, is determined not to let the tale descend into bathos. Beautifully written and elegantly constructed, *The Lovely Bones* becomes, in the words of a reviewer in the *New York Times*, 'a deeply affecting meditation on the ways in which terrible pain...can be redeemed'.

Film version: *The Lovely Bones* (2009, directed by Peter Jackson)

Read on

Lucky; *The Almost Moon*

Audrey Niffenegger, *The Time Traveler's Wife*; Jodi Picoult, *The Pact*

VIKRAM SETH (b. 1952) INDIA

A SUITABLE BOY (1993)

Commonwealth Writers' Prize 1994

Author of novels, poetry, a book about his travels in Tibet and a collection of animal fables in verse, Vikram Seth remains best-known for his epic narrative *A Suitable Boy*, first published in 1993. More than 1500 pages long in its one-volume edition (it has also been published in three separate volumes), this is the story of four families in post-independence India, all struggling to cope with their own domestic crises and dramas against the backdrop of larger political and social events. The plot revolves around the Mehra family's search for a husband, the 'suitable boy' of the title, for their younger daughter, Lata, but the book expands into a vast panorama of Indian life in the 1950s.

Everything, from private love affairs to parliamentary debates, from weddings and funerals to riots and religious festivals, has its place in the enormous narrative. Seth's ambition is endless and he marshals his characters (dozens of them) with great skill. Like a cross between a modern soap-opera and a nineteenth century novel such as *War and Peace*, his book slowly draws its readers into the world it recreates in its pages. There has long been word that Seth has been working on a sequel to *A Suitable Boy* but it has yet to be published. Indeed, in the seventeen years since his magnum opus appeared, Seth has published comparatively little. *An Equal Music*, the story of a classical violinist struggling to revitalise a love he thought he'd lost and to find artistic fulfilment through his music, was published in 1999. Otherwise his only major work is *Two Lives*, a memoir of the lives of his great uncle and aunt. It scarcely matters that he has not been prolific in recent years. His place in literary history seems secure. Few novels published in the last fifty years offer such a rich, rewarding and all-encompassing experience as *A Suitable Boy*.

🕮 Read on

An Equal Music; *The Golden Gate* (a novel in verse)
Rohinton Mistry, *A Fine Balance*

CAROL SHIELDS (1935–2003) CANADA/USA

THE STONE DIARIES (1993)

Pulitzer Prize for Fiction 1995

In a writing career that lasted from the 1970s until her death in 2003, Carol Shields produced volumes of poetry, a biography of Jane Austen, volumes of short stories and ten novels. These ranged from *Mary Swann*, the story of four very different people whose lives are linked by an obsessive interest in a Canadian poet unrecognised before her violent death, to the Orange Prize-winning *Larry's Party*, in which she uses her central character to reflect on what it might be like to be a man in a world increasingly out of tune with old-fashioned notions of masculinity. Her finest novel is *The Stone Diaries* which won both the Governor General's Literary Award for Fiction in the year it was published in Canada and the Pulitzer Prize for Fiction in the USA two years later. It is the story of an 'ordinary' woman's life from birth in rural Canada to her death in a Florida nursing home ninety years later. Daisy Goodwill Flett, as the chapter headings of the book (Birth, Childhood, Marriage, Love etc) ironically underline, lives in one sense a conventional life as (in her son's words at her memorial service) 'wife, mother, citizen of our century'. In another sense her life is most unconventional, including elements that would not have looked out of place in a magic-realist novel. Her mother dies in childbirth without even realising she is pregnant. A neighbour returns to his native Orkney and lives to the age of 115, proud of his ability to recite *Jane Eyre* from memory. And the novel in which Daisy's life is told is far from conventional. It mimics the form of a non-fiction biography with family tree, photographs of family members, excerpts from letters, journals, newspaper articles and so on. In a poignant, knowing and funny narrative, Carol Shields carefully unfolds the remarkable story of a supposedly unremarkable woman.

🕮 Read on

Larry's Party; *Mary Swann*; *The Republic of Love*
>> Margaret Atwood, *The Blind Assassin*; Jane Smiley, *Moo*

IAIN SINCLAIR (b. 1943) UK

DOWNRIVER (1991)

Encore Award 1992

For the last thirty years, Iain Sinclair has been conducting his own intense, idiosyncratic, fictional study of the topography, history and inhabitants of his adopted city, London. His work does not always make easy reading. In Sinclair's imagination there are interconnections between the most disparate phenomena and the city is a network of links between people (past and present), buildings, sites of numinous significance, books, rituals and power structures. His vision of London and his highly wrought, linguistically inventive prose make demands on the reader but the rewards are considerable. His first novel was *White Chapell, Scarlet Tracings* which followed a group of seedy and unscrupulous book dealers as they set off in search of a rare variant edition of Conan Doyle's first Sherlock Holmes story and combined their picaresque adventures with a re-imagining of the Jack the Ripper murders in the East End of London. *Downriver*, his second novel, remains Sinclair's finest achievement. The book takes as its connecting thread the story of a film crew making a documentary about the blight and ruination inflicted on the riverside by the changes of history and politics, especially the policies of the Thatcher years. But its real centre is the Thames itself and the histories it holds. *Downriver* teems with characters and stories. Stephen Hawking, Lewis Carroll, Victorian boatmen, aboriginal cricketers, 60s gangsters, wide boy dealers and a thousand other unlikely figures people its pages. Sinclair's recurring obsessions – forgotten writers from his alternative canon of English literature, Jack the Ripper, David Rodinsky and the Princelet Street synagogue, strange psychogeographical connections between different parts of the city, the churches of Nicholas Hawksmoor – all have their roles to play in creating a weirdly memorable vision of the city. Sinclair has since written some remarkable non-fiction works chronicling his journeys in and around London (*Lights Out for the Territory*, *London Orbital*) but nothing in his fiction has quite matched the rich compendium of stories past and present that *Downriver* offers.

🕮 Read on

Radon Daughters; *White Chapell, Scarlet Tracings*
>> Peter Ackroyd, *Hawksmoor*; Michael Moorcock, *Mother London*; Nicholas Royle, *The Matter of the Heart*

ZADIE SMITH (b. 1975) UK

WHITE TEETH (2000)

James Tait Black Memorial Prize (2000)

Few first novelists gain the attention that Zadie Smith did with her debut *White Teeth*. For several months before and after its publication Smith and her book were omnipresent in the media. *White Teeth* went on to win very nearly every literary prize for which it was eligible. For once the hype and the hoopla were justified. The novel is an ambitious and generous story of different generations of two families in London which takes on, with confidence and humour, the question of what it means to be English in a post-colonial world. Archie Jones is a working-class Englishman who meets Samad Iqbal, a Muslim, during the Second World War and begins a lifelong friendship with him. *White Teeth* traces the progress of that friendship through several decades, through marriage and parenthood and through the dramatically changing social landscape of post-war Britain. The story moves into the next generation with Irie (daughter of Archie and his Jamaican second wife) and the twins Millat and Magid (sons of Samad's arranged marriage). Packed with energy and inventiveness and alive with the details of London life, *White Teeth* moves back and forth through the decades to create a vivid portrait of cultures mixing and melding in the city. In the decade since its appearance, Smith has confirmed her status as one of the most exciting young writers in Britain. Two more novels have followed – *The Autograph Man*, which charts its obsessive central character's hectic pursuit of the signature of an obscure 1940s' movie star whose autograph is legendarily hard to acquire, and *On Beauty*, the story of two generations and two families of middle-class academics struggling to connect with one another. The first of these was shortlisted for the Orange Prize, the latter won it. It seems likely that Zadie Smith will be winning prizes for her fiction for many years to come.

Film version: *White Teeth* (2002, TV mini-series)

Read on
The Autograph Man; *On Beauty*
Monica Ali, *Brick Lane*; Nadeem Aslam, *Maps for Lost Lovers*; **»**
Andrea Levy, *Small Island*

READ ON A THEME: FIRST NOVELS

Tash Aw, *The Harmony Silk Factory* (Whitbread First Novel Award 2005)

William Boyd, *A Good Man in Africa* (Whitbread First Novel Award 1981)

» Jim Crace, *Continent* (Whitbread First Novel Award 1986)

Fred D'Aguiar, *The Longest Memory* (Whitbread First Novel Award 1994)

Jonathan Safran Foer, *Everything Is Illuminated* (Guardian First Book Award 2002)

Jane Hamilton, *The Book of Ruth* (Hemingway Foundation/PEN Award for First Novels 1989)

Robert McLiam Wilson, *Ripley Bogle* (Betty Trask Award 1990)

Maggie O'Farrell, *After You'd Gone* (Betty Trask Award 2001)

>> Jeanette Winterson, *Oranges Are Not The Only Fruit* (Whitbread First Novel Award 1985)

GRAHAM SWIFT (b. 1949)

WATERLAND (1983)

Guardian Fiction Prize 1983

Graham Swift has not been the most prolific of novelists (eight novels in thirty years) but his fiction, much of which explores the ways in which the past continues to reverberate in the present, is highly admired. He has won many awards, including the Booker Prize in 1996 for *Last Orders*, a deceptively simple story of four ageing men making their way from London to the coast to scatter the ashes of an old friend in the sea. His third novel, *Waterland*, had been shortlisted for the Booker thirteen years earlier and, although it didn't win, it was awarded a number of other prizes. There are many readers who would argue that it remains his most substantial achievement. It is a *tour de force* of storytelling, interweaving past and present, landscape and character, in its tale of a history teacher at the end of his tether who is haunted by the power of the subject he has spent his life studying. Set in the Fenlands, the ambiguous landscape where earth and water meet and mingle, the novel focuses on the teacher Tom Crick as he attempts, for the last time, to persuade his pupils of the importance of the past for the present. He looks back and remembers the discovery, forty years earlier, of a boy's body in a drainage ditch in the fens. In front of his bored and cheeky class, he begins thinking aloud about the reasons for the boy's death – and his monologue ranges through the history of the remote, enclosed world of the fens, the story of several generations of his own family and an account of the rivalry between his mentally subnormal brother and the boy who was found drowned. With its intertwining stories and shifting narrative, *Waterland* eventually comes to illustrate and illuminate Crick's commitment to the significance of the past.

🎬 **Film version:** *Waterland* (1992, starring Jeremy Irons as Tom Crick)

📖 **Read on**
Last Orders; *Tomorrow*
>> Julian Barnes, ***Staring at the Sun***; Peter Benson, ***The Levels***

DONNA TARTT (b. 1963) USA

THE LITTLE FRIEND (2002)

W.H. Smith Literary Award 2003

In 1992, the Mississippi-born writer Donna Tartt achieved huge critical and commercial success with her first novel, *The Secret History*, the story of a group of privileged students at an exclusive American college and their descent into bacchanalian violence. She then discovered that, in American literature in particular, there are few tasks more challenging than providing an encore to a remarkable debut. It was a decade before she finished and felt able to publish another novel. Like her first book, *The Little Friend* centres on a violent death and its consequences. The heroine, Harriet Dusfresnes, is a twelve-year-old girl in a small town in the American Deep South whose search for her brother's murderers becomes a journey into dark and dangerous territory. Robin Dusfresnes was found hanging from a tree when Harriet was a baby, the victim of a murderer who has never been caught. Unsurprisingly, his death has had a profound effect on the family. Father has left town to live with his mistress, mother has sunk into depression and Harriet's older sister, four years old at the time of the killing and possibly its only witness, has repressed all knowledge of it. Harriet has been brought up largely by her mettlesome grandmother Edie and a posse of adoring great-aunts who have encouraged her in her self-belief. Now Harriet reckons she knows who killed her brother. The murderer was one of a bunch of unsavoury rednecks called the Ratliffs. Together with her admiring sidekick Hely, she sets out to punish him. In doing so, she finds that her childish fantasies about unearthing the truth have ill-prepared her for what follows. Both a complex suspense story and a rich evocation of small town society in the Deep South, *The Little Friend* is Donna Tartt's brilliant response to the challenge of matching her first success.

📖 Read on
The Secret History

Jeffrey Eugenides, *The Virgin Suicides*; Carol Goodman, *The Lake of Dead Languages*; Joe R. Lansdale, *The Bottoms*

ADAM THORPE (b. 1956) UK

ULVERTON (1992)

Winifred Holtby Memorial Award 1992

Adam Thorpe began his writing career as a poet and his novels show a poet's sensitivity to the subtleties and nuances of language but they are not the delicate miniatures that many other poets create when they turn to fiction. For the most part they are bold and ambitious – almost epic in scale. This is true of his most recent novel, *Hodd*, a version of the Robin Hood story in which a medieval manuscript rescued from a ruined church in the aftermath of the First World War reveals a very different character to the loveable hero of the greenwoods we all know. And it is even truer of his first novel, *Ulverton*. In this book he undertakes a multi-faceted exploration of English history by means of inventing a village in the south-west, the eponymous Ulverton, and by constructing twelve very different, demanding narratives set in the village at different times in its history from 1650 to 1988. These narratives take different forms, from a seventeenth-century sermon to the TV script for a documentary about a greedy, unimaginative property developer and his battle with conservationists. The pivotal chapter of the book is probably 'Stitches', set in 1887, in which echoes of stories from the past and stories yet to come can be heard. Thorpe tells it as one long, unpunctuated dialect monologue by an aged farm labourer taking a walk around the village and recalling, often angrily, memories of class conflict and personal tragedy that places and people trigger. 'Stitches' and each of the other chapters works as an individual story but they weave together to form the longer story of Ulverton across three hundred years. The reader is shown the change and the continuity in one English community as it is shaped by time. *Ulverton* is a bravura performance, in which Thorpe recreates and re-imagines the voices of the past.

🐟 Read on

Hodd; *Pieces of Light*; *Still*
›› Graham Swift, *Waterland*

COLM TÓIBÍN (b. 1955) IRELAND

THE MASTER (2004)

International IMPAC Dublin Literary Award 2006

Born in Enniscorthy, County Wexford in the south-eastern corner of Ireland, Colm Tóibín studied at University College, Dublin and then spent several years living in Barcelona. His first novel, *The South*, drew on this experience to tell the story of an Irishwoman arriving in the city in the 1950s and embarking on a relationship with a Spanish painter. *The Heather Blazing*, the story of a Dublin judge and his troubled relationships with others, won the Encore Award for second novels. Tóibín's other novels include *The Story of the Night*, the tale of a gay man growing up and coming out amidst the dangerous politics of Argentina and *The Blackwater Lightship*, in which a young Irishman's sister, mother and grandmother struggle to deal with his AIDS-related death. *The Master* focuses on a crucial period in the life of the novelist Henry James and transforms it into a novel which went on to win the prestigious and financially lucrative International IMPAC Dublin Literary Award two years after it was published. It was an act of daring on Tóibín's part to attempt to recreate the inner life of so distinctive and unusual a man as James but he does so with great empathy and intelligence. The narrative pivots on the years when James, eager to make a name for himself in the theatre, was writing unsuccessful plays but it moves back and forth in time to include memories of James's upbringing in a high-achieving, intellectual family in New England and hints of his ambivalent, platonic relationships with other men. Henry James is renowned for the nuanced delicacy with which he delineated complex relationships in his fiction. Tóibín makes use of the same subtlety in his portrait of a man who triumphed on the printed page but found love and intimacy escaped him in real life.

🕮 Read on

The Blackwater Lightship; *Brooklyn*

Michael Cunningham, *The Hours*; David Lodge, *Author, Author* (another recent novel which focuses on Henry James); Emma Tennant, *Felony*

ROSE TREMAIN (b. 1943) UK

MUSIC AND SILENCE (1999)

Whitbread Novel Award 1999

Rose Tremain published her first novel in 1976 and was one of *Granta*'s twenty Best of Young British Writers in 1983 but it was only with the publication six years later of *Restoration*, the story of a man caught up in the amoral hedonism of the court of Charles II, that she began to attract the kind of wider attention and readership her talent deserved. She has since written novels set firmly in the contemporary world (*The Road Home*, for example, follows the fortunes of a migrant worker from Eastern Europe as he struggles with a new life in London) but she continues to be best known for her historical fiction. *Music and Silence* is set in the early seventeenth century and tells the story of Peter Claire, an English lutenist who travels from his East Anglian home to the very different world of the Danish court. King Christian IV suffers from melancholy and depression that only music seems to soothe. His estranged wife Kirsten is interested only in her German lover. Claire is haunted by memories of his failed love affair with an Irish countess, whose husband was his earlier employer, but he is drawn to one of Kirsten's maids, herself a woman in flight from her past and her family. Christian, meanwhile, seizes upon the young Englishman as some kind of potential saviour, the one person who can rescue him and the country from moral and spiritual bankruptcy. Through a variety of narrative voices, the stories of these people unfold on the page. *Music and Silence* works superbly as historical fiction, reconstructing the sights and sounds and smells of the past with great conviction, but it is also a cleverly orchestrated narrative in which Tremain can explore very contemporary ideas about love and power and the value of art.

🕮 Read on

Restoration; *Sacred Country*

Tracy Chevalier, *Girl with a Pearl Earring*; Jane Rogers, *Mr. Wroe's Virgins*

ANNE TYLER (b. 1941) USA

BREATHING LESSONS (1988)

Pulitzer Prize for Fiction 1989

Anne Tyler writes, in cool, stylish prose, of the anguish of people caught up in the pains of everyday emotional life. She is especially good on relationships: between husbands and wives, brothers and sisters, parents and children. She has been publishing her fiction since the 1960s and her novels have been shortlisted or won most of the major literary prizes in the USA. *The Accidental Tourist*, for example, the story of a travel writer struggling to rebuild his life after the death of his son and divorce from his wife, was given the National Book Critics' Circle Award for Fiction in 1985. Four years later Tyler won what is still the most sought-after prize in American literary fiction – the Pulitzer – with her eleventh novel, *Breathing Lessons*. This is the deceptively simple story of husband and wife Ira and Maggie Moran, unfolded on the single day in which they drive to the funeral of an old friend and back home. In one sense, little happens in the course of the novel. The couple bicker in the car over Maggie's wish to stop off and see their former daughter-in-law and their grandchild. They stop off for coffee and Ira is irritated by his wife's garrulous confessions of family business to the waitress. When they arrive at the funeral, they are met by the widow, Maggie's oldest friend Serena, who reveals her unconventional plans for the funeral. In another sense, such is Tyler's unobtrusive skill as a novelist that she brings to life the whole course of the Morans' marriage, its oddities and incompatibilities, their growing sense of estrangement from their children and their feelings of being out of tune with the modern world.

With unpretentious skill, ordinary lives, in all their humdrum poignancy, are illuminated (and obliquely celebrated) in Tyler's funny and insightful novel.

🎬 **Film version:** *Breathing Lessons* (1994, TV movie starring James Garner and Joanne Woodward as the Morans)

📖 **Read on**
The Accidental Tourist; Ladder of Years
Alison Lurie, *Foreign Affairs*; ❯❯ Carol Shields, *The Stone Diaries*

BARRY UNSWORTH (b. 1930) UK

SACRED HUNGER (1992)

Booker Prize 1992

Barry Unsworth has been publishing compelling and thought-provoking fiction since the mid-1960s. In 1980 his novel *Pascali's Island*, about an unscrupulous chancer working as an agent for the Ottoman authorities on a small, Greek island in the last years of Turkish rule, was shortlisted for the Booker Prize. *The Stone Virgin*, published five years later, which is set in Venice and moves back and forth in time, was also much admired by critics and reviewers. In the years since the 1980s, Unsworth has produced an array of mostly historical novels which have ranged from a sparely written narrative, half murder mystery and half fable about the nature of art, set in the Middle Ages (*Morality Play*) to a re-telling of the Greek story of Iphigenia and Agamemnon (*The Songs of Kings*). However, his most successful novel is probably *Sacred Hunger*, a sprawling, 600-page saga of the eighteenth-century slave trade, which won the Booker Prize in 1992. At the book's heart is the confrontation of two men. One is Erasmus Kemp, the son of a ruined shipowner, striving for wealth and position through the traffic in human beings. The other is his cousin Matthew Paris, a physician forced to witness the horrors of the middle passage at first-hand. Matthew is present when the maniacal cruelty of the ship's captain, Thurso, precipitates a revolt and takes part in the utopian experiment in communal living, isolated on the remote Florida coastline, which follows the mutiny. However, the enlightenment values that Matthew espouses prove fatally flawed and he is forced to the conclusion that 'nothing a man suffers will prevent him from inflicting suffering on others' but that it will rather 'teach him the way'. With its unforgiving descriptions of man's inhumanity to man, *Sacred Hunger* is an often bleak novel but it is one in which the past is brought to life with extraordinary energy and depth.

🕮 Read on

Morality Play; *The Stone Virgin*

Fred D'Aguiar, *Feeding the Ghosts*; Robert Edric, *The Book of the Heathen*

GUY VANDERHAEGHE (b. 1951) CANADA

THE ENGLISHMAN'S BOY (1996)

Governor General's Literary Award for Fiction 1996

Guy Vanderhaeghe was little known outside Canada until the appearance of *The Englishman's Boy* in 1996. A story which links Hollywood in the 1920s to one of the most infamous events in the real-life history of the Canadian West, the so-called Cypress Hills Massacre, it was published around the world and won much critical praise. At home it won the Governor General's Literary Award for Fiction, the second time Vanderhaeghe had been awarded the most prestigious of all Canadian literary prizes. The novel contains two intersecting narratives. The first is set in 1873 and follows a group of hunters who lose their horses to an Indian raiding party and then pursue the thieves into the far North where they take their brutal revenge. The second takes place in the movie industry fifty years later. Harry Vincent is a young screenwriter who is commissioned by a wealthy man intent on recreating the Old West on screen to track down an elderly survivor of the events described in the parallel story named Shorty McAdoo. As Vincent discovers more and more about the past he comes to appreciate the gulf between the reality of the West and the myths about it that the movies are busy peddling. Vanderhaeghe's other major success, which was shortlisted for the International IMPAC Dublin Literary Award in 2004, is *The Last Crossing*. This is the story of a near-saintly English gentleman and would-be missionary who has disappeared in the American and Canadian West of the 1870s while taking the word of God to the Indians. His two brothers travel from

England and enter the wilderness to search for him but nothing can prepare them for what they find there. Both of Vanderhaeghe's novels can take their places in a list of the best historical novels produced in the last twenty years.

🎞 **Film version:** *The Englishman's Boy* (2008, TV mini-series)

📖 **Read on**
The Last Crossing
Pete Dexter, *Deadwood*; Tom Franklin, *Hell at the Breech*

READON A THEME: CANADA

Margaret Laurence, *The Diviners* (Governor General's Literary Award for Fiction 1974)

Alistair MacLeod, *No Great Mischief* (International IMPAC Dublin Literary Award)

Alice Munro, *The Progress of Love* (Governor General's Literary Award for Fiction 1986)

Nino Ricci, *Lives of the Saints* (Governor General's Literary Award for Fiction 1990)

Mordecai Richler, *Solomon Gursky Was Here* (Commonwealth Writers' Prize 1990)

Richard B. Wright, *Clara Callan* (Scotiabank Giller Prize 2001)

ALAN WARNER (b. 1964) UK

THE SOPRANOS (1998)

Saltire Society Scottish Book of the Year 1998

Since the publication of his first novel, *Morvern Callar*, in 1995, the Scottish writer Alan Warner has created a fictional world that is immediately recognisable as his own: a version of his home country that is simultaneously real and surreal. That debut book, the story of its eponymous narrator, an amoral and strangely affectless young woman who embarks on an odyssey of sex and drugs and cheap hedonism when she discovers her boyfriend has committed suicide, won the Somerset Maugham Award. *The Sopranos* was his third novel. It focuses on the choir from Our Lady of Perpetual Succour School for Girls which is travelling to a competition in the big city. Orla, Kylah, (Ra)Chell, Manda and Fionnula (the Cooler) leave behind the grim port town where they live, and the depressing prospects it offers, and go in search of the bright lights for a day at least. Sex, shoplifting and the consumption of vast quantities of alcopops offer more allure than the competition which they are determined to lose anyway, since they want to be back in their local disco in time to greet the submariners on shore leave who will be invading it. Told largely through the girls' lively dialogue – part teenage slang, part Scots argot – *The Sopranos* is a vivid celebration of their brash exuberance and the vulnerability it masks. 'They've youth; they'll walk it out like a favourite pair of trainers,' as the narrative acknowledges but, for the moment, time is on their side and they are determined to waste it in the loudest, crudest and most extravagant ways they can imagine. Other writers might create such characters as these largely in order to sneer at their vulgarity but Alan Warner is on the side of his sopranos. He relishes their zest and their energy and he invites his readers to do the same.

📚 Read on

The Man Who Walks; *Morvern Callar*; *The Worms Can Carry Me to Heaven*

Jo Dunthorne, *Submarine*; Irvine Welsh, *Trainspotting*

SARAH WATERS (b. 1966)

AFFINITY (1999)

Somerset Maugham Award 2000

Sarah Waters is one of the most critically admired British novelists of her generation, chosen as one of *Granta*'s twenty Best of Young British Writers in 2003 and the recipient of many awards and prizes for her fiction. Her first three novels were all set in the Victorian era. They took many of the themes and motifs of the literature of the period and put them to new uses, creating characters and settings that her nineteenth-century predecessors firmly excluded from their fiction. Her second novel, *Affinity*, is a dark tale of nineteenth-century spiritualism and eroticism that focuses on the relationship between a repressed, upper middle-class spinster and a supposed medium imprisoned for fraud. Margaret Prior appears to be undertaking the responsibility of ministering to the needs of the less fortunate when she visits Millbank Prison, the penitentiary that once stood on the site of Tate Britain. There she meets Selina Dawes for the first time. Margaret is a troubled individual who has attempted suicide after a doomed love affair with another woman. Selina is a spiritualist and medium whose transactions with the spirit world have ended in disaster and her incarceration for fraud and assault. Yet she persists in proclaiming her belief in the existence of the supernatural and in its power over the ordinary world. Margaret is sceptical at first but inexplicable events occur. Selina seems to know everything about her new friend. The bond between the two women grows and they plan Selina's escape from Millbank but the ghosts of the past continue to haunt them as the story unfolds. Set in a brilliantly recreated world of Victorian séances and spiritualism and told through the journal entries of its two central characters, *Affinity* is a memorable investigation of the disorienting power of passion and its ability to refashion our deepest beliefs.

🎬 **Film version:** *Affinity* (2008, TV movie)

🎞 **Read on**

Fingersmith; *The Little Stranger* (a story of ghosts and social change set in Britain in the 1940s)

》 Margaret Atwood, *Alias Grace*; Tracy Chevalier, *Remarkable Creatures*; Emma Donoghue, *Slammerkin*

JEANETTE WINTERSON (b. 1959)

THE PASSION (1987)

John Llewellyn Rhys Prize 1987

Jeanette Winterson won critical acclaim and a major literary prize (the Whitbread First Novel Award) for her first novel, *Oranges Are Not the Only Fruit*. This drew on her unusual upbringing in a strict evangelical Christian family to create a liberating story of a young girl escaping the restraints of just such a background by asserting her individuality and her identity as a lesbian. *The Passion* was her third novel, published two years after her debut. Superficially a historical novel which tells of the love affair between Henri, chicken chef to Napoleon, and a cross-dressing Venetian woman called Villanelle, the book is best read as a fable or fairy tale which uses the historical background as a springboard from which to tell stories in which the ordinary and the extraordinary sit side by side on the page. It is a short book divided into four sections. In the first Henri describes his life, shaped by war and Napoleon's ambition. The second introduces Villanelle and her life in an extraordinarily vividly evoked Venice. The third depicts the meeting of these two characters on Napoleon's doomed 1812 campaign in Russia and their embarkation on an intense love affair which results in an epic journey they undertake in order to get back to Venice. In the fourth section, tragedy strikes the lovers. Henri takes the blame for the murder of Villanelle's husband and he is condemned to a prison asylum. His life has been broken by his passion but it has also been immeasurably enlarged. Filled with what in a South American novel would be called magic realism, *The Passion* isn't an historical novel in the conventional sense. In Winterson's own words, 'it uses history as invented space'. The result is one of the most imaginative novels that this most varied and inventive of writers has published.

🍃 Read on

Gut Symmetries; *Lighthousekeeping*; *Sexing the Cherry*
>> Angela Carter, *Nights at the Circus*; >> Michèle Roberts, *The Book of Mrs. Noah*

TIM WINTON (b. 1960)

CLOUDSTREET (1991)

Miles Franklin Award 1992

Tim Winton is the most admired Australian novelist of his generation and it is not difficult to see why. He began publishing his fiction when he was in his early twenties (his award-winning first novel, *An Open Swimmer*, was published in 1981) and his books have grown in their ambition and scale ever since. He has been twice shortlisted for the Booker Prize. *The Riders*, which mixes psychological suspense with a devastating love story in an account of an Australian in Ireland setting out to discover why his wife has disappeared, was on the list in 1995; *Dirt Music*, the story of an unlikely love affair between two outsiders in the wilds of western Australia, was shortlisted seven years later. *Cloudstreet* is an earlier novel than either of these two Booker candidates, a generous story of two contrasting families in Western Australia. The era is the 1940s. The Pickles have inherited a large but ramshackle house in the suburbs of Perth. The Lambs move in as tenants. The two families are very different, the Pickles boozy and bohemian, the Lambs God-fearing and uptight, but their lives gradually intertwine. Where the Lambs put their trust in the Almighty, the Pickles have more faith in Lady Luck. The Lambs, determined to triumph through hard work and 'stickability', establish a grocery store in the building which becomes a great success. 'After a time, the shop was Cloud Street and people said it, Cloudstreet, in one word.' Over the next twenty years the families are bonded together by their shared experiences of birth, death, marriage and adultery and by the memories which the house soon contains for both of them. Opening with a riverside picnic on 'one clear, clean, sweet day in a good world in the midst of our living' Winton's funny and humane novel looks back on the entwined stories which have brought all his characters to this point.

🕮 Read on

Breath; *Dirt Music*; *The Riders*

Richard Flanagan, *Death of a River Guide*; ›› Kate Grenville, *Lilian's Story*

THE PRIZES

Betty Trask Award

Betty Trask was a writer of romantic fiction who left money in her will to fund prizes to be awarded to first novels written by authors under the age of 35 in a romantic or traditional, but not experimental, style. Administered by the Society of Authors, the awards have been in existence since 1984. Some might argue that the rules have occasionally been bent in the last quarter of a century and that novels which Betty Trask herself would certainly not have considered either romantic or traditional have been rewarded but her money has gone to some excellent writers, including John Lanchester, Tobias Hill, Kiran Desai, Sarah Waters and Maggie O'Farrell.

Bollinger Everyman Wodehouse Prize

The UK's only prize specifically awarded for comic writing, this was established in 2000 and the winner is announced at the Hay Literary Festival each year. It takes its name from the comic novelist P.G. Wodehouse and from the Bollinger champagne and Everyman editions of Wodehouse books which the winner receives. Past winners have included Jasper Fforde, Will Self and Christopher Brookmyre.

Booker Prize

See Man Booker Prize

Commonwealth Writers' Prize

Organised and funded by the Commonwealth Foundation, this prize for novelists from Commonwealth countries was first awarded in 1987. In the years since then, it has been won by an array of well-known and not-so-well-known writers from Peter Carey and Earl Lovelace to Rohinton Mistry and Richard Flanagan.

Costa Book of the Year

Established in 1971 as the Whitbread Awards and taken over by the coffee company Costa in 2006, the array of prizes from which the Costa Book of the Year emerges is often seen as the Man Booker's closest rival for the position of Britain's most consequential literary award. Winners are chosen in five categories (Novel, First Novel, Children's, Poetry and Biography) and, since 1985, a panel of judges then selects the Book of the Year from the titles which have won in these categories. Novels which have won the Book of the Year include Kazuo Ishiguro's *An Artist of the Floating World*, Matthew Kneale's *English Passengers* and A.L. Kennedy's *Day*.

Costa First Novel Award

The First Novel Award has been one of the Costa Awards (formerly known as the Whitbread Awards) since 1981 when it was given to William Boyd for *A Good Man in Africa*. Other winners include Jeanette Winterson for *Oranges Are Not the Only Fruit*, Jim Crace for *Continent*, Rachel Cusk for *Saving Agnes* and D.B.C. Pierre for *Vernon God Little*.

Encore Award

There are many prizes which reward a first novel but only the Encore Award honours second novels. First awarded in 1990, the prize is administered by the Society of Authors and is given every two years. Past winners include Iain Sinclair, Colm Tóibín and A.L. Kennedy.

Geoffrey Faber Memorial Prize

Established in 1963 to honour the founder and first chairman of the publishers Faber & Faber, the prize is given in alternate years to poetry and fiction by a Commonwealth author under the age of forty. Past winners for fiction include David Storey, Timothy Mo, Trezza Azzopardi and David Mitchell.

Governor General's Literary Award for Fiction

The Governor General's Awards were the idea of John Buchan, the author and statesman, when he served a period as Governor General of Canada. They are presented annually by the Governor General to those Canadians who have achieved distinction in a number of fields from architecture to the performing arts. Seven awards go to writers, including one for fiction. In the years since Buchan established it, the Governor General's Literary Award for Fiction has become the most prestigious of all Canadian prizes for novels and short stories and has been won by nearly all the major Canadian novelists of the last few decades, including Robertson Davies, Margaret Atwood, Carol Shields and Michael Ondaatje.

Guardian Fiction Prize

Established by *The Guardian* newspaper in 1965, this prize was awarded each year until 1998 and was won by, among others, Peter Ackroyd's *Hawksmoor*, Jim Crace's *Continent* and Pat Barker's *The Eye in the Door*. In 1999 the name of the prize was changed to the Guardian First Book Award and both fiction and non-fiction debut works became eligible.

Hawthornden Prize

Amongst the oldest of British literary prizes and (rather improbably) named for the seventeenth-century Scottish poet William Drummond of Hawthornden, the Hawthornden was first awarded in 1919. It can be given to all kinds of writing from poetry to biography. Before the Second World War, winners included Siegfried Sassoon, Robert Graves and Evelyn Waugh. More recently, it has been awarded to Alan Bennett for *Talking Heads*, Antony Beevor for *Stalingrad* and, in fiction, to John Lanchester for *The Debt to Pleasure* and Hilary Mantel for *An Experiment in Love*.

Hemingway Foundation/PEN Award for First Novel

Established by Ernest Hemingway's widow in 1976 in memory of her husband and in recognition of distinguished first works of fiction, this prize can be given to either a novel or a book of short stories. Winners have included Marilynne Robinson, Bobbie Ann Mason, Louis Begley, Edward P. Jones and Jhumpa Lahiri.

Hughes and Hughes Irish Novel of the Year

Inaugurated in 2000 by the Irish booksellers Hughes and Hughes, this has since become the focus of the annual Irish Book Awards. Winners include John McGahern (*That They May Face the Rising Sun*), John Banville (*The Sea*) and Patrick McCabe (*Winterwood*).

International IMPAC Dublin Literary Award

The largest monetary prize given for a single work of fiction published in English (currently the prize is worth €100,000 to the winner), this award was created in 1996 by Dublin City Council in association with the financial company IMPAC. Novels written in any language are eligible but they must have been translated into English. Winners have included a book first published in Spanish (Javier Marias's *A Heart So White*), one in Turkish (Orhan Pamuk's *My Name Is Red*) and one in German (Herta Muller's *The Land of Green Plums*) as well as novels originally written in English such as Edward P. Jones's *The Known World* and Colm Tóibín's *The Master*.

James Tait Black Memorial Prize

James Tait Black was a publisher, a partner in the publishing firm of A&C Black in the first decades of the twentieth century. A prize in his honour was established after his death by his widow and two have been awarded, for fiction and biography, each year since 1919. Well-known writers and books that have won the James Tait Black Memorial Prize include E.M. Forster for *A Passage to India*, Winifred Holtby for *South Riding*, Graham Greene for *The Heart of the Matter*, Angela Carter for *Nights at the Circus*, William Boyd for *Brazzaville Beach* and Beryl Bainbridge for *Master Georgie*.

John Llewellyn Rhys Prize

The John Llewellyn Rhys Prize was established in 1942 by the widow of a young English writer who had been killed in action in the Second World War two years earlier and was named after him. It is awarded each year to the 'best work of literature by a UK or Commonwealth writer under the age of 35'. Previous winners include V.S. Naipaul, Margaret Drabble, Melvyn Bragg, Susan Hill, Jeanette Winterson and Matthew Kneale.

Man Booker Prize

Despite the increased attention given to awards such as the Orange Prize and the Costa Prize in recent years, the Man Booker Prize (once known simply as the Booker Prize) remains the most prestigious award for fiction in Britain. First awarded in 1969, when the winner was P.H. Newby's *Something to Answer For*, the prize has since been given to many of the best-known and most highly regarded novels of the last forty years, including William Golding's *Rites of Passage*, Kazuo Ishiguro's *The Remains of the Day*, A.S. Byatt's *Possession*, Arundhati Roy's *The God of Small Things* and Yann Martel's *Life of Pi*. The Best of the Booker, a special award given in 2008 to mark the Booker's fortieth anniversary, went to Salman Rushdie's *Midnight's Children* which had won the prize in 1981.

Miles Franklin Award

Named after the author of *My Brilliant Career*, an autobiographical novel of 1901 about a girl growing up in a rural township, the Miles Franklin Award is Australia's most prestigious literary prize. Established in 1957, using money bequeathed by Miles Franklin in her will, it was first awarded to Patrick White for his novel *Voss*. In the half century since, it has been won by an impressive array of Australian novelists from Thomas Keneally and Peter Carey to Elizabeth Jolley and Tim Winton.

National Book Award

Established in 1950, the National Book Awards are amongst the most prestigious prizes given to American writers. Although there have been other categories in the past, they are now given in just four (fiction, non-fiction, poetry and young people's literature) and are overseen by the National Book Foundation. The first winner in the fiction category was Nelson Algren for *The Man with the Golden Arm* and, since his success, the award has been given to many of the great names in American literature from William Faulkner and Saul Bellow to E.L. Doctorow and Cormac McCarthy.

Ondaatje Prize

Bearing the name of its benefactor Christopher Ondaatje, successful businessman and older brother of the novelist Michael Ondaatje, this prize is given by the Royal Society of Literature each year to the book, either fiction or non-fiction, which best evokes the spirit of a place. It replaced the Winifred Holtby Memorial Prize which, between 1967 and 2002, was awarded to the best regional novel of the year.

Orange Prize

First awarded in 1996, the Orange Prize for Fiction has attracted controversy from the start but has also established itself as one of the most prestigious of British literary prizes. The controversy has usually focused on the fact that it is only open to women. It is awarded each year to a female author of any nationality for the best novel written in English and published in the UK in the preceding year. Some writers, both male and female, have claimed that such positive discrimination is unnecessary in the modern literary world and at least one distinguished *grande dame* of fiction, A.S. Byatt, is on record as believing that the prize is sexist. Her publishers have been instructed never to submit her books for it. Despite the arguments about its validity, the Orange Prize has an excellent track record of picking out deserving winners which have included Carol Shields's *Larry's Party*, Andrea Levy's *Small Island*, Zadie Smith's *On Beauty* and Marilynne Robinson's *Home*.

PEN/Faulkner Award for Fiction

After he won the Nobel Prize for Literature in 1949, William Faulkner used the prize money 'to establish a fund to support and encourage new fiction writers'. One of the eventual consequences of Faulkner's generosity was the establishment thirty years later of this award, run in association with the writers' organisation International PEN. The first winner was Walter Abish for his novel *How German Is It*. Recent winners have included Philip Roth's *Everyman*, Kate Christensen's *The Great Man* and Sherman Alexie's *War Dances*.

Premio Strega

The best-known and most prestigious literary prize in Italy, the Premio Strega was first awarded in 1947. It has been won by very nearly every major Italian writer of the past seventy years from Alberto Moravia and Giuseppe Tomasi di Lampedusa to Primo Levi and Claudio Magris.

Prix Goncourt

One of the longest-established and most famous of all literary prizes, the Prix Goncourt emerged from the Académie Goncourt, an organisation founded in 1900 with money bequeathed by the writer and publisher Edmond de Goncourt. Each year since 1903 a ten-member board of the Académie has chosen a novel to receive the Prix Goncourt. The first winner was the now extremely obscure John Antoine Nau but, over the years, the prize has been won by many famous French writers, including Marcel Proust, André Malraux, Simone de Beauvoir and Michel Tournier. In winning the Goncourt, an author achieves glory before financial reward (the prize is a mere 10 euros), although sales of the winning novel in France are always so enormous that victory is also guaranteed to increase his or her bank balance substantially.

Pulitzer Prize for Fiction

Joseph Pulitzer was born in Hungary in 1847 and, after an adventurous youth, settled in the USA in the late 1860s. He became a wealthy newspaper publisher and, when he died in 1911, he left money in his will to establish a series of prizes for achievement in journalism, literature and music. The Pulitzer Prize for the Novel was first awarded in 1918 to *His Family*, a now obscure work by a writer named Ernest Poole. Over the next thirty years it was won by a number of other novels which have long since been forgotten but it was also awarded to books which have survived rather better, including Edith Wharton's *The Age of Innocence*, Margaret Mitchell's *Gone with the Wind* and John Steinbeck's *The Grapes of Wrath*. Since 1948, the award has been known as the Pulitzer Prize for Fiction and has been given to such giants of American literature as Ernest Hemingway, William Faulkner, Harper Lee, William Styron, Norman Mailer, Alice Walker, Toni Morrison, John Updike and Philip Roth.

Richard and Judy Best Read of the Year

For the six years of its existence, the Richard and Judy Book Club, run in conjunction with the TV chat show hosted by Richard Madeley and Judy Finnegan, was one of the most effective means ever devised for promoting books to the British public. Books chosen for the club were almost guaranteed a large increase in sales. One of the club's spin-offs was the Richard and Judy Best Read of the Year, an award voted for by members of the public and handed out at the annual British Book Awards.

Saltire Society Scottish Book of the Year

The Saltire Society was founded in 1936 and one of its aims is to preserve and encourage Scottish cultural achievements in all the arts. It sponsors a number of awards in different fields. The Scottish Book of the Year award was established in 1995, when it was given to William McIlvanney for *The Kiln*, and it has been won by, among others, Andrew Greig's *In Another Light*, Kate Atkinson's *Case Histories* and A.L. Kennedy's *Day*.

Somerset Maugham Award

Somerset Maugham gave money in 1947 for the establishment of a prize to be awarded each May to the British writer or writers under the age of thirty-five adjudged to have produced the best book of the previous year. The money from the award is to be spent on foreign travel. The prize is now administered by the Society of Authors. In the past it has been won by Kingsley Amis, Ted Hughes, John Le Carré, Julian Barnes, Carol Ann Duffy, Rachel Cusk and Maggie O'Farrell.

Whitbread Book of the Year
See Costa Book of the Year

W.H. Smith Literary Award
Founded by the book retailer W.H. Smith in 1959, this award was given every year from 1959 to 2005, when it was discontinued, to the author of a book of particular merit. Originally, potential winners had to be writers from the UK or the Commonwealth but this rule was later relaxed so that US authors and the authors of works in translation could be considered. The last three winners of the award (Donna Tartt, Richard Powers and Philip Roth) were all American. Other winners over the years included Laurie Lee for *Cider with Rosie*, Jean Rhys for *Wide Sargasso Sea*, Doris Lessing for *The Good Terrorist*, Vikram Seth for *A Suitable Boy* and Ted Hughes for *Tales from Ovid*. The W.H. Smith Award for Fiction was a short-lived prize which ran in parallel with the W.H. Smith Literary Award for several years at the beginning of this century.

Winifred Holtby Memorial Prize
See Ondaatje Prize

INDEX

Other books in the 100 Must-Read Series

Discover your next great read ...

100 Must-Read American Novels
Nick Rennison, Ed Wood
9781408129128

100 Must-Read Books for Men
Stephen E Andrews,
Duncan Bowis
9780713688733

100 Must-Read Classic Novels
Nick Rennison
9780713675832

100 Must-Read Crime Novels
Nick Rennison,
Richard Shephard
9780713675849

100 Must-Read Fantasy Novels
Stephen E Andrews, Nick Rennison
9781408114872

100 Must-Read Historical Novels
Nick Rennison
9781408113967

100 Must-Read Life-Changing Books
Nick Rennison
9780713688726

100 Must-Read Prize-Winning Novels
Nick Rennison
9781408129111

100 Must-Read Science Fiction Novels
Nick Rennison, Stephen E Andrews
9780713675856